Ravishing DisUnities

WESLEYAN POETRY

Edited by Agha Shahid Ali

RAVISHING

DisUnities

Real Ghazals in English

Afterword by Sara Suleri Goodyear

Wesleyan University Press

Published by University Press of New England :: Hanover and London

Wesleyan University Press

Published by University Press of New England, Hanover, NH 03755

"Introduction," "Ideas of Order in an Afterword," "Basic Points about the Ghazal," and this collection © 2000 by Wesleyan University Press

Printed in the United States of America

5 4 3 2 1

Library of Congress Cataloging-in-Publication Data

Ravishing disunities : real ghazals in English / edited by Agha Shahid Ali ; afterword by Sara Suleri Goodyear.
   p. cm. — (Wesleyan poetry)
   ISBN 0-8195-6438-9 (alk. paper) — ISBN 0-8195-6437-0 (pbk. : alk. paper)
   1. Ghazals, American. I. Agha, Shahid Ali, 1949-   II. Title. III. Series.
   PS593.G44 R38   2000
   811'.5408—dc21   00-009342

"Frazzle" from *AFTER ALL: Last Poems* by William Matthews. Copyright © 1998 by the Estate of William Matthews. Previously published in *ACM (Another Chicago Magazine)*. Reprinted by permission of Houghton Mifflin Company. All rights reserved.

Acknowledgments

John Balaban's "Locust Ghazal-Dazzle" is reprinted by permission of Copper Canyon Press from *Locusts at the Edge of Summer: New and Selected Poems* by John Balaban. Copyright © 1997 by John Balaban.

Keki Daruwalla's "Partition" first appeared in *Ariel*.

Faiz Ahmed Faiz's "Southern Lovesong," translated by Andrew McCord, first appeared in *Modern Poetry in Translation*.

Mirza Asadullah Khan Ghalib's "Elegy for the Poet's Nephew Arif," translated by Andrew McCord, first appeared in *Paris Review*.

John Hollander's "Ghazal on Ghazals" is reprinted by permission of Yale University Press from *Rhyme's Reason: A Guide to English Verse* by John Hollander. Copyright © 1989 by John Hollander.

William Matthews's "Frazzle" is reprinted by permission of Houghton Mifflin from *After All : Last Poems* by William Matthews. Copyright © 1998 by William Matthews.

W. S. Merwin's "The Causeway" first appeared in *The River Sound*, copyright © 1999 by W. S. Merwin. Reprinted by permission of Alfred A. Knopf, a division of Random House, Inc.

Heather McHugh's "Ghazal of the Better-Unbegun" is reprinted by permission of Wesleyan University Press/University Press of New England from *The Father of the Predicaments* by Heather McHugh. Copyright 1999 by Heather McHugh.

Isabel Nathaniel's poem "Summer Whites" first appeared in *POETRY*, was copyrighted in 1998 by The Modern Poetry Association, and is reprinted by permission of the Editor of *POETRY.*

Elise Paschen's "Sam's Ghazal" is reprinted by permission of Story Line Press from *Infidelities*, by Elise Paschen. Copyright © 1996 by Elise Paschen.

Sagaree Sengupta's "Soup" first appeared in *The Annual of Urdu Studies*.

David R. Slavitt's "Ghazal" is reprinted by permission of Louisiana State University Press from *PS3569.L3* by David R. Slavitt. Copyright © 1998 by David R. Slavitt.

Judith Taylor's "Famous Pairs" first appeared in her chapbook *Burning*, published by the Portlandia Press in 1999.

Ann Townsend's "Ghazal of the Winter Storm" originally appeared in *Pleiades,* and is reprinted by permission of the author.

for Qafia Radif & all the other poets in this book

Contents

Afterwords

Ravishing DisUnities

Introduction

For a seemingly conservative, but to me increasingly a radical, reason—
form for form's sake—I turned politically correct some years ago and
forced myself to take back the gift outright: Those claiming to write gha-
zals in English (usually American poets) had got it quite wrong, far from
the letter and farther from the spirit. Of course, I was exercising a Muslim
snobbery, of the Shiite elan, but the ghazal floating from so many month-
lies to quarterlies was nothing of the kind. And wasn't the time ripe for
stringent, formally tight disunities, not just arbitrary ones?

First, to be teasingly petty, I offered the pronunciation: *ghuzzle*, the *gh*
sounding like a cousin of the French *r*, the sound excavated near unnotice-
ably from deep in the throat. So imagine me at a writers' conference
where a woman kept saying to me, "Oh, I just love guh-zaals, I'm gonna
write a lot of g'zaaals," and I said to her, in utter pain, "OH, PLEASE DON'T!"
When I complained to Carolyn Kizer (as a translator of Urdu poets, partic-
ularly Faiz Ahmed Faiz, she is aware of the real thing) that the Americans
had got the ghazal quite wrong, she, in extravagant despair, responded:
"Have they ever!" For those brought up on Islamic literary traditions, espe-
cially the Persian and Urdu ghazal, to have many of these arbitrary near-
surrealistic exercises in free verse pass for ghazals was—is—at best amus-
ing. And let me assure the free-versifiers that nothing neo-formalist lurks in
my true-to-form assertions.

Then, I had to register a protest, an irritation at Paul Oppenheimer's as-
sertion that the sonnet is "the oldest poetic form still in wide popular
use"; he cites its origins in thirteenth-century Italy. But the ghazal goes
back to seventh-century Arabia, perhaps even earlier, and its descendants
are found not only in Arabic but in—the following come spontaneously to
mind: Farsi, German, Hebrew, Hindi, Pashto, Spanish, Turkish, Urdu—and
English. The model most in use is the Persian (Farsi), of which Hafiz
(1325-1389)—that makes him a contemporary of Chaucer's—is the ac-
knowledged master, his tomb in Shiraz a place of pilgrimage; Ghalib
(1797-1869) is the acknowledged master of that model in Urdu—the only
language I know whose mere mention evokes poetry. Lorca also wrote
ghazals—*gacelas*—taking his cues from the Arabic form and thus citing in
his catholic (that is, universal) way the history of Muslim Andalusia. And,
as Raymond Scheindlin has written, "The typical medieval Hebrew love

1

poem belongs to a genre known in the Arabic literary tradition as *ghazal*," which "flourished primarily in Andalusia from the 11th to the 13th centuries"—that is, in Muslim Spain.[1]

Finally, I found it tantalizing to strike a playful pose of Third-World arrogance, laced with a Muslim snobbery (I hope no one will accuse me, as an editor once did, of playing some kind of wise sage from the East). For a free-verse ghazal is a contradiction in terms. As perhaps a free-verse sonnet, arguably, is not? At least those who arrive at free verse sonnets have departed from somewhere: from Petrarchan platforms or Elizabethan terminals (as all the ghazals in this volume, even when not entirely true to the canonical form, reveal departures from a definite place—for example, Paul Muldoon's *sui generis* "double" ghazal). I mention the sonnet because the ghazal—somewhat arbitrarily—has been compared with it. But imagine a sestina without those six words. What would be the point? Many American poets (the list is surprisingly long) have either misunderstood or ignored the form, and those who have followed them have accepted *their* examples to represent the real thing. There have been no points of departure. But, as the *Princeton Encyclopedia of Poetry and Poetics* informs us, the ghazal was introduced to Western poetry "by the romanticists, mainly Fr. Schlegel, Rückert, and von Platen (*Ghaselen*, 1821) in Germany, and was made more widely known by Goethe, who in his *Westöstlicher Divan* (1819) deliberately imitated Persian models."

So what is the Persian model—I mean the real thing? I will plagiarize from *The Practice of Poetry* (edited by Robin Behn and Chase Twichell), in which my not altogether correct entry, "Ghazal: The Charms of a Considered Disunity," quite correctly argues:

> Because such charms often evade the Western penchant for unity—rather, the unities—I offer a truly liberating experience: the ghazal. . . . When students ask about a poem such as *The Waste Land*—How does it hold together?—I suggest a more compelling approach, a tease: How does it not hold together? I underscore *How* to emphasize craft. The ghazal has a stringently formal disunity, its thematically independent couplets held (as well as not held) together in a stunning fashion.[2]

The ghazal is made up of couplets, each autonomous, thematically and emotionally complete in itself: One couplet may be comic, another tragic, another romantic, another religious, another political. (There is, underlying a ghazal, a profound and complex cultural unity, built on association and memory and expectation, as well as an implicit recognition of the human personality and its infinite variety.) A couplet may be quoted by itself without in any way violating a context—there is no context, as such. One should at any time be able to pluck a couplet like a stone from a necklace, and it should continue to shine in that vivid isolation, though it would have a different lustre among and with the other stones. In less exotic terms, the poet must have no enjambments between couplets.

Then what saves the ghazal from what might be considered arbitrariness? A technical context, a formal unity based on rhyme and refrain and prosody. All the lines in a ghazal can *appear* to have—because of the quantitative meters of Persian and Urdu—the same number of syllables; to establish this metrical consistency, poets follow an inner ear rather than any clearly established rules, as in English. To quote the Marxist historian Victor Kiernan—a translator of Iqbal and Faiz, two of Urdu's most important poets:

> Urdu metres, mainly derived from Persian, are varied and effective. They are based on a quantitative system which divides the foot into sound-units composed of long vowels and vowelized or unvowelized consonants. Urdu has, properly, no accent; on the other hand, Urdu verse, evolved for public declamation, can be recited with a very strong accentual rhythm, the stresses falling on almost any syllable in accordance with the quantitative pattern. This pattern cannot be reproduced with much fidelity in English, where quantity plays a considerable but an undefined and unsystematic part, and where two "long" (or "strong") syllables cannot be made to stand side by side in a fixed order, as they do habitually in Urdu verse.[3]

However, some rules of the ghazal are clear and classically stringent. The opening couplet (called *matla*) sets up a scheme (of rhyme—called *qafia*; and refrain—called *radif*) by having it occur in both lines—the rhyme IM-MEDIATELY preceding the refrain—and then this scheme occurs only in the second line of each succeeding couplet. That is, once a poet establishes the scheme—with total freedom, I might add—she or he becomes its slave. What results in the rest of the poem is the alluring tension of a slave trying to master the master. A ghazal has five couplets at least; there is no maximum limit. Theoretically, a ghazal could go on forever (in practice, poets have usually not gone beyond twelve couplets).

Perhaps one way to welcome the shackles of the form and be in emotional tune with them is to remember one definition of the word *ghazal*: It is the cry of the gazelle when it is cornered in a hunt and knows it will die. Thus, to quote Ahmed Ali, the "atmosphere of sadness and grief that pervades the ghazal . . . reflects its origin in this" and in the form's "dedication to love and the beloved. At the same time, the form permits, in the best Persian and Urdu practice, delineation of all human activity and affairs from the trivial to the most serious." Further, although there is no unity in the form "as there is in European verse, atmospheric and emotional cohesion and refinement of diction hold the poem together, permitting at the same time terseness, intensity, and depth of feeling, uniqueness of imagery, nobility of language, and a high conception of love" in its unconnected couplets. For the "outstanding mood of the ghazal," in Urdu and Persian, has remained "melancholic and amorous."[4]

Of course, most of the poets who have contributed to this anthology have not been particularly in tune with this emotional aspect of the ghazal. Rather, they have been intrigued with the form, and it is gratifying to find that most of these contributors usually work in open, not given, forms. What, then, led them to try this thematically freeing but formally shackling form? Kelly Le Fave, one of the poets represented here, has this to say:

> In a ghazal, one is not allowed to hide rhymes in enjambments or vary the refrain; the pressure that some traditional forms demand to delicately manage rhymes or refrains is off, since the repetition of the *qafia* and *radif* in a ghazal is both frequent and emphatic. Once I decide on a refrain, I make as large a list as possible of rhyming words—which is great fun—and spend days letting them incubate in my head, waiting to light on surprising variations in my approach to the inevitable resolution of each couplet. In fact, so much is given in the form—the regular syllables of the lines, the absence of enjambment, the disunity of one couplet's relation to another, the thematic address to the absent beloved, the rhyme and refrain—that what is left to the poet once the scheme is established is solely the inventive delight of the momentary that I think so many poets crave. As someone who writes mainly in a lyric free verse mode, I find the ghazal offers a fascinating and fresh combination of brief lyric moments contained within strict structural restrictions. These restrictions, along with the obligation to avoid unity, create—unexpectedly—a liberating ground within which the lyric voice has the ability to shine and accumulate without requiring a larger narrative or thematic meaning. What pleases in a ghazal is the variety with which a conspicuous sameness can be sustained; what the form unleashes is the poet's mercurial powers.[5]

The question asked again and again: Is there no unity of any kind except the formal one? To cite Elizabeth T. Gray, Jr.'s introduction to *The Green Sea of Heaven: Fifty Ghazals From the Díwan of Háfiz*:

> These ghazals are often puzzling to the "Westerner" who approaches them for the first time. . . . The poems do not seem to go anywhere: there is . . . no ultimate resolution or answer. [The couplets] seem unrelated to one another. And everything seems ambiguous: is the poet talking to the one he loves? Or is he approaching a patron? Or is this a nugget of wisdom at the disciple who seeks union with God? If the poet is talking about his beloved, is the beloved a man or a woman? Is it actually the poet talking?

The thirst for unity haunts the "Westerner," even in these fussingly nonlinear days. So to repeat the question: Is there no unity? The answer: Well, no. However, there is a cultural unity—created by the audience's shared assumptions and expectations. There is a contrapuntal air.

The first convincing approximation of the form in English—at least for our times—is John Hollander's:

> For couplets the ghazal is prime; at the end
> Of each one's a refrain like a chime: "at the end."

Having seen or heard this opening couplet, one would know that the *radif* is "at the end" and the *qafia* a word or syllable that would rhyme with "ime." Thus the second line of every following couplet will end with "at the end" preceded IMMEDIATELY by a rhyme for "ime." Hollander continues:

> But in subsequent couplets throughout the whole poem,
> It's this second line only will rhyme at the end.

He goes on with thematically autonomous couplets:

> On a string of such strange, unpronounceable fruits,
> How fine the familiar old lime at the end!

> All our writing is silent, the dance of the hand,
> So that what it comes down to's all mime, at the end.

> Dust and ashes? How dainty and dry! We decay
> To our messy primordial slime at the end.

> Two frail arms of your delicate form I pursue,
> Inaccessible, vibrant, sublime at the end.

> You gathered all manner of flowers all day,
> But your hands were most fragrant of thyme, at the end.

> There are so many sounds! A poem having one rhyme?
> —A good life with a sad, minor crime at the end.

> Each new couplet's a different ascent: no great peak
> But a low hill quite easy to climb at the end.

> Two armed bandits: start out with a great wad of green
> Thoughts, but you're left with a dime at the end.

Each assertion's a knot which must shorten, alas,
This long-worded rope of which I'm at the end.

To mark the end of the ghazal, often a poet has a signature couplet (*makhta*) in which s/he can invoke his/her name pseudonymously or otherwise. Hollander, charmingly, pseudonymizes:

Now Qafia Radif has grown weary, like life,
At the game he's been wasting his time at. THE END.

Notice that with the exception of the first (well, in this case also the second) and final couplets, the poem would not in any way suffer by a rearrangement of the couplets. Nor would the ghazal suffer if one would simply delete some of its couplets. Such freedoms may bewilder, even irritate, those who swear by neo-Aristotelianism and New Criticism.

Hollander has done something remarkable here, for by having "at the end" as his *radif* he has caught the particular spirit of the form. For, "within the ghazal, the poet almost always adopts the stance of a romantic hero of one kind or another: a desperate lover intoxicated with passion, a rapt visionary absorbed in mystic illumination, an iconoclastic drunkard celebrating the omnipotence of wine."[6] In this century, especially among left-wing poets, the poet is often the committed revolutionary intoxicated with the struggle for freedom. "He represents himself as a solitary sufferer, sustained by brief flashes of ecstasy, defined by his desperate longing for some transcendent object of desire," which may be "human (female or male), divine, abstract, or ambiguous; its defining trait is its inaccessibility." (This form, in other words, which as it is being described in English would seem to lend itself comfortably to "light" verse, is anything but, and that is bound to be a challenge for those attempting it in English.) What is particularly compelling about Hollander's "at the end" is that it contains the possibility of being imbued with such longing and loss!

Of course, the past has seen *some* attempts in English at the formal properties of the ghazal. Here is James Clarence Mangan's "The World: A Ghazel":

To this khan, and from this khan
    How many pilgrims came and went too!
In this khan, and by this khan
    What arts were spent, what hearts were rent too!
To this khan and from this khan
    (Which, for penance, man is sent to)
Many a van and caravan
    Crowded came, and shrouded went too.

Christian man and Mussulman,
    Guebre, heathen, Jew, and Gentoo,
To this khan, and from this khan,
    Weeping came, and sleeping went too.
A riddle this since time began,
    Which many a sage his mind hath bent to:
All came, all went; but never man
    Knew whence they came, or where they went to.

Mangan has other examples, but all of his seem to have little more than historical interest. I recently discovered another example, in James Elroy Flecker's 1922 play called *Hassan*. There it serves largely to enhance the play's love theme:

How splendid in the morning glows the lily; with what grace he throws
His supplication to the rose: do roses nod the head, Yasmin?

But when the silver dove descends I find the little flower of friends,
Whose very name that sweetly ends, I say when I have said, Yasmin.

The morning light is clear and cold; I dare not in that light behold
A whiter light, a deeper gold, a glory too far shed, Yasmin.

But when the deep red eye of day is level with the lone highway,
And some to Meccah turn to pray, and I toward thy bed, Yasmin.

Or when the wind beneath the moon is drifting like a soul aswoon,
And harping planets talk love's tune with milky wings outspread, Yasmin,

Shower down thy love, O burning bright! for one night or the other night
Will come the Gardener in white, and gathered flowers are dead, Yasmin!

This is a particular kind of ghazal, a continuous one (though the couplets are still separate), which is called a *qata*. But that is always the exception that emphasizes the customary ghazal in which each couplet is an autonomous poem.

An aside: After a few years of relishing Hollander's ghazal and popularizing it among my poet-friends and students, I wrote to him with a few suggestions: "All the lines of a ghazal must have the same syllabic length, and in yours though most have twelve syllables, some lines have eleven and one has thirteen and one has ten." When I wrote this, I had not paid attention to Urdu's quantitative meters. Hollander answered: "I had not intended in my example, partially because of needing the stress-pattern to make the rhyming audible in English, to observe the strictest syllabic integrity (my lines had a four-stressed, largely anapestic rhythm, but a few iambic substitutions allowed for the divergent syllable-length on some occasions.)" These words have proved instructive for me. As a result, my suggestion to those attempting ghazals in English is that they create some system whereby some basic—but not debilitating—consistency in line lengths (inclusive of the *qafia* and *radif*) is established.

One essential ingredient missing in unrhymed ghazals is the breathless excitement the original form generates. The audience (the ghazal is recited a lot) waits to see what the poet will do with the scheme established in the opening couplet. At a *mushaira*—the traditional poetry gathering to which sometimes thousands of people come to hear the most cherished poets of the country—when the poet recites the first line of a couplet, the audience recites it back to him, and then the poet repeats it, and the audience again follows suit. This back and forth creates an immensely seductive tension because everyone is waiting to see how the suspense will be resolved in terms of the scheme established in the opening couplet; that is, the first line of every succeeding couplet sets the reader (or listener) up so that the second line amplifies, surprises, explodes. For example, if Hollander were to recite:

> You gathered all manner of flowers all day,

the audience would repeat it and so on, and then when he'd come to

> But your hands were most fragrant of thyme . . .

the audience would be so primed, so roused by this time that it would break in with "at the end" even before Hollander would have a chance to utter the phrase. And then, in raptures, it would keep on *Vaah-Vaah*-ing and *Subhan-Allah*-ing. If the resolution is an anticlimax, the audience may well respond with boos. I should mention that a ghazal is often sung. Some of the great singers of India and Pakistan have taken ghazals and placed them gently within the framework of a raga and then set the melodic phrase (which contains the individual lines of the ghazal) to a *tala* (cycle of beats). The greatest of them all was Begum Akhtar, who died in 1974. This seemingly "light" form can lead to a lot of facile poetry (haiku-ish-ly, one could say). But in the hands of a master? Ghalib's ghazals reveal a great tragic poet, Faiz's a great political one.

To make abundantly clear why an unrhymed ghazal would be a contradiction in terms to an Urdu or Persian speaker, I will offer some of my own ghazals. A time for confession: When I attempted my first ghazal, I totally dispensed with the *qafia* and settled simply for the *radif*: That is, I made matters much too easy for myself, despite Hollander's compelling example. This is what I did:

> The only language of loss left in the world is Arabic.
> These words were said to me in a language not Arabic.
>
> Ancestors, you've left me a plot in the family graveyard—
> Why must I look, in your eyes, for prayers in Arabic?
>
> Majnoon, his clothes ripped, still weeps for Laila.
> O, this is the madness of the desert, his crazy Arabic.
>
> Who listens to Ishmael? Even now he cries out:
> Abraham, throw away your knives, recite a psalm in Arabic.
>
> From exile Mahmoud Darwish writes to the world:
> You'll all pass between the fleeting words of Arabic.
>
> The sky is stunned, it's become a ceiling of stone.
> I tell you it must weep. So kneel, pray for rain in Arabic.
>
> At an exhibition of Mughal miniatures, such delicate calligraphy
> Kashmiri paisleys tied into the golden hair of Arabic!
>
> The Koran prophesied a fire of men and stones.
> Well, it's all now come true, as it was said in the Arabic.
>
> When Lorca died, they left the balconies open and saw:
> his *qasidas* braided on the horizon into knots of Arabic.
>
> Memory is no longer confused, it has a homeland—
> Says Shammas: Territorialize each confusion in a graceful Arabic.
>
> Where there were homes in Deir Yassein, you'll see dense forests—
> That village was razed. There is no sign of Arabic.
>
> I too, O Amichai, saw the dresses of beautiful women—
> And everything else, just like you, in Death, Hebrew, and Arabic.

And now for my *makhta*:

> They ask me to tell them what Shahid means—
> Listen: It means "The Belovéd" in Persian, "witness" in Arabic.

Sometime later I made another attempt, dropping some of the couplets, adding some, revising others, but it is a more honest attempt. My choices were dictated by my not wanting to let go of the *makhta* of the earlier version, which on a couple of occasions in New Delhi had drawn for me the requisite *VahVahs*. Keeping that in mind, I created my *matla*:

> A language of loss? I have some business in Arabic.
> Love letters: calligraphy pitiless in Arabic.

Here are some couplets that correspond with couplets in the first version:

> Majnoon, by stopped caravans, rips his collars, cries "Laila!"
> Pain translated is O! much more—not less—in Arabic.

> At an exhibit of miniatures, what Kashmiri hairs!
> Each paisley inked into a golden tress in Arabic.

> When Lorca died, they left the balconies open and saw:
> On the sea his *qasidas* stitched seamless in Arabic.

> Where there were homes in Deir Yassein, you will see dense forests—
> That village was razed. There is no address in Arabic.

> I too, O Amichai, saw everything, just like you did—
> In death. In Hebrew. And (Please let me stress) in Arabic.

> Listen, listen: They ask me to tell them what Shahid means:
> It means "The Belovéd" in Persian, "witness" in Arabic.

I think it is the seeming arbitrariness of the unrhymed ghazal that has kept it from being a necessary part of the American "mainstream" (a word around which quotation marks, in any context, are wise); it has led only to "exotic" dabblings. I think many Americans are often tempted by the "wisdom" of the East. One has only to remember Tagore, Gibran, Ravi Shankar, Maharishi Mahesh Yogi . . . I am being unfair, but only to make the point that when they heard that an ancient culture sanctions a poem of thematically independent couplets, various surrealistic juices overflowed. It is the sort of thing that happens with haiku (Richard Howard is supposed to have said that as a poetry editor having to read five hundred haikus a week was like being nibbled to death by goldfish, and James Merrill in his "Prose of Departure" has actually used rhymes for his haikus so that Americans would know that "something is going on").

Further, there is a bonus for those willing to pursue the real ghazal (in addition to not having to search for titles—"Ghazal" suffices; and because the word is now found in *Webster's Third International Dictionary*, there is no need to italicize). Through ghazals, English can again employ full rhymes, even the most cliché-ridden, without apology or embarrassment because the *radif* enables the rhyme to lose, through a transparent masking, its strained and clichéd element; the *qafia* is made transparently invisible. What an incredible gift: all those rhymes one thought could never be used again. Further, the ghazal also offers English a chance to find a formal way, a "legal" way out, to cultivate a profound respect for desperation—something that American poetry has not altogether lost. As for the English? Let me leave it there.

I do like many aspects of the so-called ghazals by many American poets (among the more vibrant examples, I would single out James Harrison, Adrienne Rich, Robert Mezey, and Galway Kinnell) and could make a case for their discarding of the form in the context of their immediate aesthetics and see in their ghazals a desire to question all kinds of authorities by getting away from linearity and that crippling insistence on "unity." I have certainly enjoyed Rich's and W. S. Merwin's translations of Ghalib's ghazals. Now while translating an Urdu or Persian ghazal into English, one would have to use free verse (it would be impossible to sustain a convincing *qafia*—given the *radif*—when translating couplet after couplet; however, Andrew McCord in his translation of Ghalib in this anthology may well be proving me wrong). Anyway, I found their translations, like Elizabeth T. Gray, Jr.'s of Hafiz, rather attractive because they often struck me not just as efforts but real accomplishments. But when poets attempted their own original ghazals, they simply did not bother with the form. I have a suspicion that Aijaz Ahmad did not quite establish the primacy of the form when explaining Ghalib to those who collaborated with him in translating Ghalib. Thus, this is how Adrienne Rich explains the form in a note to her "Ghazals: Homage to Ghalib":

> This poem began to be written after I read Aijaz Ahmad's literal English versions of the Urdu poetry of Mizra Ghalib (1797–1869). While the structure and metrics of the classic *ghazal* form as used by Ghalib are much stricter than mine [But hers are not strict at all!], I adhered to his use of a minimum five couplets to a *ghazal*, each couplet being autonomous and independent of the others. The continuity and unity [Notice how it becomes difficult to get away from "unity"] flow from the associations and images playing back and forth among the couplets in any single *ghazal*.[7]

Perhaps the business of rhyme and refrain just did not suit the aesthetic politics—and the political complexion—of various contexts in the late sixties and early seventies? The ghazal, as many of those poets practiced it,

gave them the authority of a foreign and rich culture; it allowed them for-
mally to question the authority of their own culture's often rigid proscrip-
tions, and perhaps they saw in the thematic freedom of the couplets a
chance for all kinds of liberation. What would have been paradoxical to
many Westerners—the ghazal's blend of "unity and autonomy"—would
have attracted them. (I hope it is clear that my use of "West" and "Western-
ers" assumes immensely deconstructive qualifications; Edward Said argues
there is no such thing as the "West." This may be an apocryphal story, but
Mahatma Gandhi upon being asked what he thought of Western civiliza-
tion is supposed to have answered, "It would be a good idea." I must add
that there is no such thing as the "East" either.)

I love forms, but I do not wish to come across as some kind of rheu-
matic formalist. I am not, certainly not the neo-kind who wishes to save
Western civilization—with meters and rhymes! However, the issue here is
that by following the form of the ghazal, the writer could find herself tan-
talizingly liberated, surprising herself with unusual discoveries by being
stringent with herself as she goes from one theme to another in couplet
after couplet. Form has been associated (remember the recent free verse
vs. formalism debate)—and quite wrongly, really—with what holds truth
back, especially political truth. But as Faiz said, there is nothing good or
bad in any poetic form but the poet makes it so. And he used this very
strict form to express an impassioned left-wing politics—using the stock
figure of the Beloved to figure as the Revolution. Martha Zweig, one of the
poets represented in this anthology, offers this provocative aside:

> Beloved-revolution is happiest in the ghazal, where it has been able to rise to
> the occasion of Faiz's bright insight as sort of found-object of the tradition;
> once you see it, you've got it made, it's a cinch, over and over, because it al-
> ways was, and remains, objectively(!) *there*. Although the meaning of the
> beloved-revolution metaphor has everything to do with obsession, these
> poems do not at all resemble sestinas, for example; I testify further that ses-
> tina—even maddened over a capricious beloved—cannot be the name of
> *this* tune. The sestina wants to control; it hopes to spellbind in its ritual; it
> stakes a claim in its six magic words and interweaves them ever more
> densely and narrowly, like the web of a funnel spider. The sestina is out to
> get you, its plot thickens. The Revolution might write sestinas about *us*, but
> never vice-versa![8]

In comparison, however, "the ghazal's couplets are quixotic, each takes
another tilt at the poem's material; the speaker flirts, beguiled into the
next and the next couplet by the will-'o'-the-wisp glimmer of the last."[9]

So how far can one go with those free verse couplets with nothing but
a seeming arbitrariness to guide one? In January 1996, some months before

his death, I was discussing the ghazal with Larry Levis at Warren Wilson College in North Carolina. He was ready to attempt some real ghazals, saying of the ones in various magazines that one finds a juxtaposition of things among them but the poet does not seem to have a way to return—as a musician in a jazz solo does. The jazz soloist has a way of coming back no matter how far he has gone: because of an underlying melody, a basic rhythm. Thus, readers of the free-verse ghazal cannot but ask how the couplets are connected: they will automatically be looking for thematic unities. That is why I think the free verse ghazal in America (or anywhere else) seems always a momentary exotic departure for a poet, nothing that is central to him or her, to their necessary way of dealing with the world of their poetry. But the actual form, by its very nature, erases that expectation, preempts it. Recite Hollander's ghazal to anyone and notice how no one will ask for unities; the form seduces one into buying the authority of each couplet as thematically autonomous. When poets go crazy with the idea of composing thematically independent couplets in a free-verse poem, they manage to forget what holds the couplets together—a classical exactness, a precision so stringent that it, when brilliant, surpasses the precision of the sonnet and the grandeur of the sestina (I do mean that) and dazzles the most untutored of audiences. The ghazal's disconnectedness must not be mistaken for fragmentariness; that actually underscores a profound cultural connectedness. The ghazal is not an occasion for angst; it is an occasion for genuine grief.

So while I admire the effects of various "ghazals," it really is time the actual form found its way into American poetry. It really is. For one thing, as the narrator of *Swann's Way* phrases it, one can exact from a restriction a further refinement of thought, "as great poets do when the tyranny of rhyme forces them into the discovery of their finest lines." If one writes in free verse—and one should—to subvert Western civilization, surely one should write in forms to save oneself *from* Western civilization?

Notes

1. Philologos, "On Language," *Forward* (March 14, 1997), 10.
2. Robin Behn and Chase Twichell, eds., *The Practice of Poetry* (New York: Harper Perennial, 1992), 205.
3. Faiz Ahmed Faiz, *Poems* (London: Allen & Unwin, 1969), 15. The quote is from Victor Kiernan's introduction.
4. Ahmed Ali, *The Golden Tradition* (New York: Columbia University Press, 1973), 2–22.

5. Kelly Le Fave, letter to author, October 10, 1999.

6. Shamsur Rahman Faruqi and Frances W. Pritchett, "Lyric Poetry in Urdu: In the Ghazal," *Delos* (Winter 1991): 7.

7. Adrienne Rich, *Poems: Selected & New, 1950–1974* (New York: Norton, 1974).

8. Martha Zweig, letter to author, March 7, 1998.

9. Martha Zweig, letter to author, March 7, 1998.

The Ghazals

On Location in the Loire Valley

Clouds of mistletoe hang in the poplars, which can't survive.
Still, decorated with ruin, they enchant our lives.

In stone castles, cold's steel roars straight up the spine,
and, shivering to the core, we decant our lives.

For one minute of dead quiet, the restlessness stops.
"Room tone." Sound men record the silent rant of our lives.

Together we consort with chance, cascade through time.
Each trip we find ourselves on the gallivant of our lives.

After a whole life in miniature: naive start, work, friends,
even a small death at the end, we adjourn to the constant of our lives.

How we stumble at goodbyes, as if we felt nothing for no one,
and heartless to the bone. Quiet meals, quick farewells dismantle our lives.

At home, we regale loved ones with adventures half-true.
Night drives through fog nonchalant as our lives.

Along with legendary art, herding sheep at St. Michel,
the wizardries of smell . . . all was banter in our lives.

The heart has a curfew. We can tell folk where and how we were,
but we cannot tell them who. What a pantomime, our lives.

Not the shadow family we became, not the shiver beneath the smile,
not the people who clung to us in the mad canter of our lives.

The Hollywood Version

A chorus line hoofer goes on for the sleek but tight star.
"Stop the presses!" yells the editor of *The Grove Heights Star*.

Tin Pan Alley hacks tinkle the ivories, Yuletide tunes.
Atop a tinseled Christmas tree twinkles a snow-white star.

The small-town doctor shouts, "Quick, boil water, lots of water!"
The sheriff hands the deputy his bloody but bright star.

The GI from Brooklyn whistles at a pinup and winks.
A tousled toddler wishes at window: "Star light, star . . ."

A cast of thousands in a sundry olden armor follows
The holy man on horseback who points toward a midnight star.

Ghazal for Garcia Lorca

Still you came back knowing you must die in Granada,
intricate, tricky, disapproving, prying Granada.

One hand grips the collar, the other sounds the pocket.
They make no room for the shameless or the shy in Granada.

The fingers still point. The smiles always know.
Everything seemed to me about to cry in Granada.

The steep cobbled streets and cobblestones dewed by the cold,
late snow cradled in valleys against the sky in Granada.

The sketches stitched by your big sister into cushions,
A bus I might have taken but didn't try in Granada.

The guitar hot from the lathe, the leather ottoman,
all I wanted but had no room to buy in Granada.

Walking at night my sandals marked me American—
no one goes out in less than a coat and tie in Granada.

No one above contempt. I'll never visit the caves.
I missed you every place and never knew why in Granada.

I felt at home, how home is hard with cruel people,
home even the Gypsies leave, waving goodbye in Granada.

An absinthe glass, a slope clouded in rhododendron,
corroded-copper colored tile that caught my eye in Granada.

An Oh, an Ay, a consolation we could wander
hand in hand with, Garcia Lorca and I, in Granada.

Sleep of Leaves

In fall woods-water, a woman tastes sleep of leaves.
Father's green death-eyes closed in a waste: sleep of leaves.

Like koi, the red-gold of maples swims in wet grass.
She wishes fish would not be in haste: sleep of leaves.

Her baby's sweat smells of milk: rain clings to the fern.
Nursing, baby curves into the chaste sleep of leaves.

Seed-winds play with her baby's dandelion hair.
Seed-play can't reach her father's encased sleep of leaves.

Absorbed in poems, her baby's cry pulls her out.
Diane can't live for long in the laced sleep of leaves.

Locust Ghazal-Dazzle

While summer lingers late in trees,
locusts try to orchestrate the trees.

Their shrill cantatas tumble through the shade
upon a boy alone and staring up at trees.

Alone with himself, listening for a voice,
he hears the whine of insect wings in trees.

Buried long and mute beneath the ground
they rise up through the branches of the trees.

A canopy of song between dark earth and sky
spills out sunlight and kindred calls in trees.

Ghazal of Paradise

All lost strands come home in Paradise;
Does flesh talk to bone in Paradise?

Time may line and wear the fairest face;
Rent seams are one in Paradise.

Signs of age fade out without a trace;
Each soul will be toned in Paradise.

That said, we'll take our pleasure twenty ways,
begin again full grown in Paradise.

Come, Desire, take us in your embrace;
Let sweet angels moan in Paradise.

No form of love's a sin within that place.
Why should we atone in Paradise?

Forget the wings; we'll dress in silk and lace.
The second coming's well known in Paradise.

Sing, you angels, heaven's earthly grace;
We'll not carol alone in Paradise.

Enchantment

Gold fringe I've always eyed it. It's ravishly afraid,
and jewelry tangled, silly—its very light flees afraid.

It's the beach's winter. Tannish, dead-hair palm fronds.
You hummingbirds, stop puckering, you never leave afraid.

Long ago my old friend murdered, utterly . . . so in September,
shattered and still, the murderous dreams fall on me, afraid.

Her moans can't stop this meager tale. The beasts are brutish;
She startles, whitens. I love her more when she's afraid.

He's at the almost-bearing-up stage. "Travel incognito,"
his visions with small paws and wings say, and "Don't be afraid."

A feathered ear and the whitest wrist. They vanish with the lies.
The swan has only tulle for cover. She even preens afraid.

He'd write XXX with Molly O darling come couldn't I
be like her Nora shivering violets freely afraid.

My Memoir

X has written an unauthorized autobiography.
—J. D. McClatchy

Lately, all my friends say, "I'm writing my memoir."
The phrase has a certain cachet: *in my memoir* . . .

At the precise moment of my birth Havana crowed—
all the roosters in unison (so I'll say in my memoir).

The thirteenth fairy arrived at my christening with gifts:
Be-ribboned attributes all here on display, in my memoir.

My parents rocked me in a warm cats-cradle of laced arms—
Every night, Brahms-lulled, I still sway in my memoir.

We played with lightning in my grandfather's big house;
after the accident, there was hell to pay in my memoir.

I won gold medals in dream events at the Olympics;
there's a breathtaking play-by-play in my memoir.

Later, in college, I avoided conventional humiliations
with an aplomb that bordered on blasé, in my memoir.

Everything I owned could be packed neatly in one suitcase—
From the baby grand down to my negligee, in my memoir.

I starred in my share of wild affairs and sad intrigues:
Paris. The Seventies. But I don't care for exposé in my memoir.

For a dizzying decade I pedaled through marriage and career—
Credentials which I modestly downplay in my memoir.

Least Wicked Stepmother and Most Promising Perfectionist—
I can't help but mention the two (touché!) in my memoir.

My own infanta's birth was graced with doves and portents;
See how she grows taller in every way, in my memoir.

This part is true: I write in sleep with my fountain pen—
The sheets are streaked with indigo by day, in my memoir.

My house is haunted by a blue-green imago and a ghost
whose silver saxophone still plays and plays, in my memoir.

At my funeral, the eulogies to Blake were deeply affecting.
People were so bereft, I decided to stay, in my memoir.

Says the Prophet

That unhappy belief hounds us from birth.
It begins with the womb, ends in the earth.

The heel of Achilles (not his courage, not his heart)
The only measure of his human worth.

Beloved Marilyn, like Christ, like Lazarus, Monroe
Rises from death moldy about the skirt.

Buy low, sell high, death (you must have one) my commodity
of choice (cash the only treasurable girth).

Big questions, like departmental meetings, like bad sex,
Leave the survivors longing for mirth.

Poetry is too often declared dead (like the
Hymen, it's noticed only for its dearth).

In Hell's oval office sings Virgil, mimicked by Boswell.
(It's history they desire to unearth.)

Czechoslovakian Blues

Goodnight my love, see you tomorrow then.
Where in the world will we be tomorrow then?

You'd think a map could designate our lost-ness
If x is now, the spot of our sorrow, then.

The rakish wind is snapping through the branches—
Their prayers go forth like little fedoras then.

Of what does she dream? The reddest reddest thing?
So much depends upon that wheelbarrow then.

I watched sleepily the flakes, as if their sheer
Weightlessness, whites drift could make me follow them—

Rain turns ice to water in Prague's dark gutters;
So Karen is bound to suffer now and then.

The Nightingale

Some men say I've forgotten why I sing,
as if I were a happy, careless thing.

But just my speechless body stayed behind—
my memories rose too as I took wing.

My new heart beats a hundred times a minute,
as my old one did when I was weeping and pleading.

My new tongue is whole, but small and hard,
my beak is one more wound I keep reopening.

And out come pain and bitterness and sorrow,
but men say, Hear how beautifully she sings.

The song I paid so much for is a bird's—
wordless, yes, but marvelous with meaning.

Immortal bird, that is, condemned to fly
forever through the trees from spring to spring.

Young lovers hope to hear me for good luck—
charmed by my beauty, slow to feel its sting.

By then I've flown to other eager listeners
oblivious to the truth of what I sing.

Those few who understand lose heart themselves,
and wish they hadn't heard the news I bring:

My name before and still is Philomela.
Music pours out, I remember everything.

28

Drowning Ghazals

1
(first line by Charles Simic)

there was a movie theater here once
a bar over there where we drank beer once

I remember your feet cold in the bed
how we loved in front of the mirror once

before all this drowning we were so young
didn't you kiss my neck in Kashmir once

there was a time when this nearly slayed you
I saw your eyes hollowed raw by tears once

but that was long ago your *saison d'enfer*
was there a movie theater here once

2
(first line by Emily Dickinson)

After all the Birds have been investigated and laid aside
After we with our Bellies are sated and laid aside

Soon enough the lozenge Moon will dissolve into the dawn
Your Ponytail will be unbraided and laid aside

The Drowned will rise up like Afterthoughts Brushstrokes
The Fishermen will weep their Hooks unbaited and laid aside

The Blind will find their ways somewhere else with their Fingertips
The Hours will shiver when Morning is created and laid aside

The last time you called my name *Denver* out across the dark
there was Nothing I had I wouldn't have traded and laid aside

3

(first line by John Ashbery)

we thought the sky would melt to see us
that stars would ash and plea *please empty* us

we thought at the very least the moon
would stay still and quit trying to flee us

you were unhinged and suddenly squealing
you drowned and said we could no longer be us

this year's horses are wild unbroken
these birds are lame and unharmonious

you tore up notes my sudden verses
while I believed I would somehow free us

New England

In the beginning were the Words of God, disguised as stones:
like hard, black irises dropped in the faithful's eyes, these stones.

Waves hunched in worship shake the granite shore beneath my feet
as once it shuddered under the soles that colonized these stones.

Salt of the earth, they said, "Let nothing grow upon this spot
till hell silts over. Let them lie among blowflies and stones."

No schist for me, no strata resurrected from dead tongues.
I'll cleave to coal and shale and strive to anglicize the stones.

Cursing a blue streak when his plow beached on a granite spur,
the farmer wiped his brow, letting his sweat baptize these stones.

"Fuck you, you fucking fucker," froths a four foot gradeschool kid,
thrilled to outdo his friends, who've grown curt, coarse, streetwise, like
stones.

Such meditation on the inner life: the CAT scan's Ommm;
unearthly images of what metastasized as stones.

Who doesn't long to blame someone for their infirmities?
I turn to God and nature, but their alibis are stones.

Feldspar and granite, raised up from platonic depths, are cold
against my back and, like the ghostly new moon, rising stones.

The Jackal sings his privy business to the world at large.
Hungry, unfit to kill, he grumbles lullabies to stones.

What Is a Poem?

A motive for talk show hosts to ruminate at century's end:
the primp before an extra-special date at century's end.

Feature films comprised solely of long shots and close ups,
sociopolitical hullabaloos that will not abate at century's end.

Back at the homestead, a life-or-death game of hide-and-seek,
the tempest that forces our mission to wait at century's end.

One's naked baby shitting sweetly on one's living room sofa.
(New holidays so loved ones can fornicate at century's end.)

Ohmigod, you're never gonna believe this! and its reply.
Finding an inner sanctum to dephlegmate at century's end.

Neither the mother lode nor the quagmire it's hidden beneath,
but the absence of pre-fab community gates at century's end.

A need to agree with both headmaster and student body?
Regardless, the timekeeper will long to be late at century's end.

Robert Nicholas Casper by any other name.
A ringing true and a turning towards fate at century's end.

The Anonymous Lover

Like a phantom I've pursued your guise from the beginning,
cupped in your hands my own heart like dice from the beginning.

Was I wrong to have so fallen for your indifferent heart,
providence misguiding me with lies from the beginning?

I kneel to pray but see that far away look on your face,
some say love like death pulls a knife from the beginning.

Wafted into clouds let my words die if they fly nowhere,
when in your heart are grafted my eyes from the beginning.

The past, present, and future, wear their indifferent gaze,
friends leave, turn enemies, say the wise from the beginning.

This loneliness that has grown like a vine in a crevice,
having nothing to reach, gently sighs from the beginning.

I wake from a dream, seeing your face skating on water,
I touch knowing your untouched state flies from the beginning.

In a pool of mirrors, we're minnows pretending to be whales,
I'm nameless as a shadow of your cries from the beginning.

Game of Logic

If you wish the prophesies to bare their logic,
ask the worldly do they ever spare their logic.

The housing of our thoughts needs no doors or windows,
you may touch a glass fruit but you can't pare its logic.

The force of light drives the dark into its fervor,
what we hold of passions simply flare their logic.

In time our hurts hide like vagabonds on a train,
but in memory scars always wear their logic.

True yogis trap the world in a cup of water,
people pass by mocking but won't share their logic.

So don't entice us into your strange game, Logic,
for we must pretend we are fair to our logic.

House of a Nautch Girl

In the petalled night, I swing in my glitter,
like moths come ashore you wing in my glitter.

What drives you to the cageless flesh in my limbs,
is the want that thrones you king in my glitter.

I dance, you clasp the vapor of my sighs,
I'm reachless to all you bring in my glitter.

By your brief lust, I'm the shush of cunt and tits,
but like fools you hide your ring in my glitter.

On my island, squeal your wants, bask in my gig,
pigs with a vain enchanted thing in my glitter.

Well

Not all the poems will be set in Israel in the end.
My pen will drink from the American well in the end.

In the desert my ancestors were guided by smoke and fire.
From atop City Hall, William Penn has me under his spell in the end.

What began with begging to be heard in English
Has come to whispering up the strairwell in the end.

The bedrooms are dark, the children are asleep,
But their dreams will be swept away by the real in the end.

My lamp is their inheritance. My heart, too.
They'll hear its fond farewell in the end.

In the beginning, I created a material world.
The rabbi's words gave it a soul in the end.

In my coffin, for my heart, a little bag of soil.
Dying in the Diaspora turned out swell in the end.

Their poems are being written, the children's, as I speak.
It's the way we make a home of exile in the end.

Though *Torah* was spoken nightly at our table, He never appeared
Who had promised to share our meal in the end.

The bus ride to center city is short, safe and cheap.
Not so the journey underground to Israel in the end.

In the beginning, a slap startled the hand that delivered it.
To fill the hole, they used the back of the shovel in the end.

The year recycles endlessly, but I am never renewed.
I wear the same shroud to crawl or sail in in the end.

I came to the fortune teller to receive the future.
It is they, my foes and enemies, who fall in the end!

Not all the poems need be set in Israel. Wherever we travel,
Our sorrow will be sweetened by a sip from Miriam's Well in the end.

Dream

Every morning she empties themes of him.
Even now she empties her dreams of him.

An oriole comes to sugar water.
Through the window she watches gleams of him.

The sun climbs the fig vine, the quilt burns her.
Showering, her pouts are (she steams!) of him.

Hot words make her gut tie up with anger.
She'd cut him to ribbons—long streams of him.

He is loving, he is violent or sweet.
Her hands sore, holding the extremes of him.

She thinks it is her fault when his back hurts.
She suffers when his pain drives screams from him.

They used to dialogue their hopes and wants.
She has them still—his writing—reams of him.

She lies reading her detective novel—
Her thoughts, while eating chocolate creams, of him.

Does anyone ever know the other?
She thinks she knows now all, it seems, of him.

And Clements, do you think that she is you?
Even now you are filling dreams of him.

Night

Now she's alone and on meds in the night.
The sound of weeping spreads in the night.

She stands at the window amazed at the stars.
They spin through a curtain of threads in the night.

She watches her children, angelic, asleep.
She's tucked them into their beds in the night.

By now their dreams are of winter and snow.
The snowmen are dancing with sleds in the night.

Outside, the trees lost their leaves in the wind.
A carpet of gold and reds in the night.

But the kids have all grown and left their toys.
Her meaning in life cut to shreds in the night.

How will she function, how adjust?
Life without children is what she dreads in the night.

But Clements, her story—there's more than you know.
Time collapses—Death treads in the night.

Marriage

What's lost in love? What retrieved? It could be
we lose ourselves to make love what could be.

He offers water, but I want to burn
the night down. I ask where the Glenlivit could be.

Night tricks from its air cloth he slips into.
Does he keep just arms up those sleeves? That *could* be.

Eye of grosgrain, button of palest shell
hanging on thread's delicate *could* be.

My spine shivers open along the zipper's teeth:
the touch withheld, air softer than velvet could be.

He unfastens darkness, unhooks me down to skin—
he never knew how elusive light could be.

His is the hand that undoes me at last.
His undoing's all I conceived night could be.

As pearl is to mother, mortal heart to cage,
grain's nubbins are to the sheaves: what could be.

Even the most fragile bud troubles forth,
caught open early, to bear the bright, cold bee.

Touch of a thief on a tiny catch. I'm sprung,
taken by promise's predicate: could be.

What have I got? Words to undo the heart with
a wink and a whisper: *It is, Sweet*, not *Love, it could be.*

Canyon

They fall against their rising, cliffs undone
by weather and what weather's left undone.

Sunk at canyon bottom, the road scales
its arched body into lift undone.

And I run within a thunder's pulse
that lights me through, flickering off and on.

What haven't I done? Wind strips the oaks. Limbs
strain at root, by their wild heft undone.

Even the sky can't stop. It gnaws itself,
black cloud undone by black, unloosened one.

What can I do but let the storm trouble
eye and blood, the heart at wrist undone?

Until it's passed, moving me between
nerve and fault. I resist. Undone,

the coal's consumed by its own breath. No rain.
Just trembling air. Sky's whip. The passion done.

Home

When I was young I couldn't wait to leave home
and then I went away to make the world my home.

In England a poet's wife suggested "heimweh" for what I felt—
German for homesickness even when you're home.

The agoraphobe and claustrophobe respectively
cannot bear to leave or stay inside their home.

Our day-old son wrapped in a blanket in your arms
and I'm in the car waiting to take both of you home.

Mortgage means "dead pledge." To buy a house
You need one. A house can be mistaken for a home.

It won't be hard to name the poet who wrote a sonnet sequence
about his mother and father. He called it "The Broken Home."

A shovel, rake, and pick axe hang inside my neighbor's garage.
Like a god he has ordered the chaos of his home.

Never let me forget: colliers mind coal. Michael's an angel.
In heaven as on earth the coal of grief warms the soul's home.

Ghazal

When I turned to say something the presence was gone.
Sand in the palm of an open hand is an essence gone.

The road ended. I found the map was untrue or the sand
had shifted. When will I find where the lost road's gone?

Blink of an eye—Thursday in Douz and the market is busy;
Bedouins dressed like Old Testament shepherds—and the present is gone.

Of course it's true, the Sahara's an ocean, waves of sand—
but look, I dip in my hand and the ocean is gone.

Rose crystals blossom in Chott el Djerid, the sand's crude
sculpture rising where the water rises, a mirage, and then is gone.

Phoenix dactylifera, a poet's tree! *Doigts de lumière*
I hold my hand up to block the sun and the sun is gone.

Quick sand? Don't struggle, move slowly. The guidebook
reports, it takes hours before you're completely gone.

When the desert inside me matched the nothingness beyond,
I recited my name, and the presence was gone.

Hers

Without her, we forget. But our dreams blaze with her.
All of us, who spent our early days with her.

Bears touch budding breasts, tongues touch tongues.
Oh to be the water, the way it plays with her.

Sand is stretched taut, like white sheets.
Rising sea comes on with moon. It sways with her.

All the liqueurs in the house, banana, orange.
And oh, the talk, even in that sweet haze with her.

A room, a bed, a chair. Her failing flesh.
What she held, what held her, loosens, grays with her.

Once, in a green place, she became us all.
Then she became herself. But being stays with her.

Mary and Martha, she said, as if they were sisters.
She named her Martha. But Mary is always with her.

Now

One eye reads "Born then," the other "Dead now"—
Between them I'm alive, I'm dead some time now.

O'Hara and Crane won't grace the lectern today.
I'd sell their jaundiced-eared volumes for a dime, now.

The price of getting some's gone presidential.
Deceit, petty theft—*my* little crimes now.

You won't kiss? Refuse any kind of condom?
You'll do. Please do. We're falling, falling to grime now.

Damn the young he-beauties, they tigerwalk
on what might have been my prime. Now

God's voice comes, goes like the last, the next high:
"Steven, come, come—the sublime's now."

Consider

A child stares at the wall for hours,
understanding Creation in less than 4 hours.

A dog twitches, calm quiver from sleep,
as dawn approaches, signaling more hours.

Sand crabs dig to escape from the water.
The tide follows neither rules nor hours.

Are considerations too slippery to see?
Is there ever anything but pain or hours?

The thick swell of a tongue rolls back.
What is left to consider? These are war hours.

Katherine means "pure," as in "God" or "girl";
I do not recognize my own name or face for hours.

Everyone Wants the Earth

The packed tissue-box of a peony explodes: visible time.
Like the sun's flames, it arrives in waves of time.

The scent of spring roses. Reawakening volcanoes.
Like us, the earth flowers slowly through time.

A single flower unfolds the world in pulsing waves.
All growth points to a new terrain. Beyond: only time.

Everyone wants to tell the earth how it must be saved;
No one wants to hear the planet thinking time.

Flattened by world's sheer size, we run fast.
We'd rather be dwarfed by space than time.

Tornadoes and quakes can't shake us from this small piece of time.
Yet we slip easily into evolution. We can't feel its time.

Earth listens to our painful progress and tries
To loosen us to breathe in waves, in time.

With the beauty we have been fleeing.
Oh Rachel, catch up. Stop. Only let time.

Partition Ghazals

1

This may pass muster and yet may not pass:
This past we are talking of is not the past.

This may pass muster and yet may not pass.
The past is heavy on our shoulders, good it is the past.

Tenses curve and coil through the murk of time—
The past erupts except that it is not the past.

Beyond the linear and hence beyond the line
The magic lantern images of memory flash past.

Gandhi's egg-shell head, round as a shrunken sun,
Has it set for ever into a black-hole past?

Not that Gandhi looked the only anchorite.
Jinnah looked ascetic too—how the years passed!

This should pass muster, and yet may not pass.
All tenses are tricky, especially the past.

The lesson for you, wine-bibbling Kaikhusroo—
The past you talk of may not have been the past.

2

Freedom was a lamp that was lit before our eyes.
A forest of shadows that stood serried, massed.

Suddenly broke rank and fled, we don't know where.
How could a flame spark off such a storm blast?

Yet flame and shadow live and die like lovers:
Lip touching lip, the hands firmly clasped.

But must we live through it again? Won't colors fade
On memory's dark edge, why do they hold fast?

Sword and sickle pounce on the caravan's edge.
Who has been abducted? Who saw that woman last?

His classic suits replaced by bone-hugging *achkans*,
Which made him look tall though he was shriveling fast.

Are they mere ghosts now, symbols, forgotten penons
fluttering atop a fog-bound, creaking mast?

Writing—Painting:

> I go where it's blue.
> —William Gass

Splotches blotched among blue,
what words match red, wrong blue.

Peacock shimmy. Memory's sky.
Shapes insist: stories sung blue.

Choose everything: waterfall avenue;
cerulean roof drops flung blue.

Robin's eggs, unhatched, fly up;
orange drowns tongue blue.

Gone to pick berries. Be back
by two, hands stung blue.

Graze this shaggy bush for knowledge
of the good—having clung blue.

Irresistible—this erratic caress;
hair shaken wet, hung blue.

Past desert's edge—plum trees;
off the plain of Sharon—the sea rung blue.

Ghazal of an Island

San Francesco del Deserto

St. Francis came here by mistake, driven to land by the sea
discharging the storm's orders, on a muddy strand by the sea.

When the weather cleared, it was lovely—vines and cypresses,
a garden ready for tending, for a florist's hand by the sea.

Boys and girls once rowed here, to dance their reels and hear
squeezebox and timbrel, a hot medieval dance band by the sea.

Basta! said Francis to the birds that chattered as he prayed.
And they held their peace, obeying his command by the sea.

He plunged his walking stick in the fertile earth, a recent
cutting he had trimmed. It took root, a magic wand by the sea.

Father Antonio shows me around. "Here's where he prayed"—
and a waxy statue still prays where old walls stand by the sea.

A monk, in blue jeans, trims hedges with gas-powered clippers,
motor buzzing with gray fumes the wind has fanned by the sea.

Across the lagoon, a man in boots walks on the water,
bending to dig clams where mud bands expand by the sea.

For Laurie

Here, in the café where raucous songs blare, the white wine
calms me down. When will you get here to share the white wine?

We'll take our time by the water, birds chirping behind leaves
as other voices ebb and flow: your red hair, the white wine.

If we get a little drunk and start to kiss, or make out
like teenagers, we can blame the scent you wear, the white wine.

If your blouse comes undone, we'll take a full bottle home
and you'll dab your nipples—I'll sip there the white wine.

We'll leave the windows open to stir the gauze curtains
and take off our clothes, naked as the air, the white wine.

But I could get drunk on a boat on calm water, so you'll
be enough for this buzz—as good as (I swear) the white wine.

After a while at sea, you feel the waves even on land,
like your love an ocean away. It's a prayer, the white wine.

And just as I smuggled you into my dark hotel room, once,
when we finally pass customs, we won't declare the white wine.

Of the Tides

Atlantis is a name for the future, although the tides
rise and subside at will. As the moon goes, so go the tides.

If the city, one day, is submerged, and not paved over,
it won't be like an aquarium, with towers below the tides.

You can tell by the mud banks in the lagoon, where the sun
fires its glaze: the city will surface—when out flow the tides.

The beauty of water is its pulsing. It pulls back
only to prepare a swollen punch, a flush blow, the tides.

Then it drops back again, leaving the doorways dripping, pools
shimmering on paving stones, antiphony of yes and no, the tides.

Ghazal of the Lagoon

Morning, on the promenade, there's a break in the light
rain here in the serene republic. I take in the light.

Every walker gets lucky at this gaming table,
where the gondoliers, like croupiers, rake in the light.

Through the glare of a restaurant's window, I see
fish glinting, like spear points that shake in the light.

I could sit on the edge and get wet forever,
all to consider a speed boat's wake in the light.

Furnaces burn. We sweat until we shine, fired up
by the wavy vases glassblowers make in the light.

Row me out, friars, in your *sandolo* on the waves
that glitter like ducats, for God's sake, in the light.

Night Sounds

By the time I enter the gorge, it's dark, although voices
call from somewhere. Who's calling? It's hard to know voices.

All night long, the hubbub continues, but so far off I can't
make out any words. All the tugs on the river tow voices.

It's too dark to pitch a tent. I lie awake on a sleeping bag,
listening for the hidden ventriloquists who throw voices.

Through the night, every noise represents a secret vote:
birdsong or mimicking signal; cries, barks, or low voices.

The dark comes in layers: a shimmery cloak of sky, plush clouds,
needles, broad leaves, eyelids—and behind each shadow, voices.

I think of a naked woman with Bach in the choir loft,
shadowed at evening, a harmony that needs no voices.

When the wind picks up, dark angels must be rehearsing,
a plainsong of moaning vowels in soprano voices.

The Weekend

You mow the back yard and I'll rake. Then wax the floor, down
on your knees, while I swab the toilet. Mark another chore down.

Is this any way to spend a weekend? Better to kick back
and watch the Dolphins go deep—complete!—a new set of four downs.

Or send the children to a neighbor for the afternoon.
Like kids, I'll drop my shorts if you pull your underdrawers down.

It's Sunday, a day of relief, but Jehovah's Witnesses
and then a tag-team of Mormons practically knock the door down.

Sometimes I'm so close to tears, it's hard to look out the window
at the back yard, to remember what the storm tore down.

Why don't the missionaries try something new? "Have you received
Rilke into your life? His elegies might help you when you're down."

Clouds move in. The grass out back is agitated by a school
of quick shadows. Soon, I hope, the heavens will pour down.

Baseball

We're swatting fungoes. Jimmy swings, and there goes the baseball
up up over the fence. That's how we lose the baseball.

I shower too late. Red splotches cover my legs and hands
from poison ivy that holds, in its shadows, the baseball.

Just before sundown, when a batter conks a high fly
above trees, the sky's transparent—and so's the baseball.

Every good pitcher spins mysteries, hiding the clues, the grip
of fingers. Batters hammer him when he shows the baseball.

It's boring in right field, so I swat away gnats and look
at a rising dot until it falls and my glove swallows the baseball.

"Go to hell, Babe Ruth," yelled the Japanese soldier on the beach,
tossing his grenade the way an outfielder throws the baseball.

A Southern Ghazal

Moscow, October 1978

What, sometime, did not pass before these eyes?
How bright the alley was when she did rise . . .

Before good people with time enough from sorrow to ask
After any sufferer under the spinning skies.

Cold sets in so firmly the era is forgotten
When the rose would bud, bloom, turn in the breeze.

When there were more lovers than strangers
Days passed tolerably sitting together with enemies.

Now it can hardly be grasped but before, in span
Of a glance, worlds passed by at the lifting of these eyes.

—translated from the Urdu by Andrew McCord

For a Poetess

Many the nights that have passed,
But I remember
The river of pearls at Fez
And Seomar whom I loved.
—"Laurence" Hope, 1903

The corners of the frontispiece yellow from their darker edges.
Aching eyes lift in tremolo from their darker edges.

Moon lit your blood in the jasmine-blooming gardens;
bodies still glide in tableau from their darker edges.

Your "hungry soul" laps at the page with its "burning, burning":
your moans send out an echo from their darker edges.

The river shores still remember a note of your tribute,
drifting on lovers' cast shadows, from their darker edges.

Silk covers your lips, your voice, your fingers, your arms.
Your black lines weave a trousseau from their darker edges.

Wind is striking the palm trees where you walked;
fronds shake like tousled arrows from their darker edges.

Your nights spread quiet over "parched and dreary" sand.
A Finch fills them till they glow from their darker edges.

Sensations Upon Arriving

The swallows fold themselves into sheets of solid air. In silent films
dust lifts from the field. Light crackles as it does everywhere in silent films.

From black peat-bricks in the fireplace, a concentrated odor—
like a dog's footpads—wafts clean and rare in silent films.

And the depraved scent of dove's dung: in a bowl two flowers
perfume even the water with light—*luminaire*—in silent films.

The wind snatches thistle-seeds. The rooks go by flapping as wildly
as eyebrows when actors pretend to be scared in silent films.

Before the treeline, the familiar river wrinkles. Rain
streaks the window by lightning-glare, in silent films.

Entering the room, he sees the spectacle of his own absence, how the
world
will be. And stands frozen, the way they stare in silent films.

Moon and Page Ghazal

Before the neutrinos could interact with matter, they went out.
His voice hardened. The foreplay went out.

Through a pocked sky he dragged her by the rope in her mouth.
She didn't like it. When he opened the door, her stray went out.

To wound him no deeper than to awaken him, she thought.
Under eaves, the buzzing of mud daubers in their piped clay went out.

That could not be his meaning, on two legs walking backward.
But whoever heard her pray went out.

Only a fly responds to a moving hand in thirty milliseconds.
Biting the hole in her lip as each day went out.

They met at the footsteps of the altar, in a groined chamber of salt.
Forever, she said—*flash*—smiling as the bridesmaid went out.

Ghazal

lazm tha ke dekho mera rasta koi din aur

Should you not look after me another day?
Why did you go alone? I leave in only another day.

If your gravestone is not erased first my head will be.
Genuflecting at your door, in any case, it's me another day.

Yesterday you came and now you say, "Shall I go today?"
Okay. It's not forever, but it was for, surely, another day.

As you left you said to me, "We'll meet on Judgment Day."
That's rich! After this destruction could there be another day?

In my house you were the fourteenth night of the moon.
Why this dark house? Wane slowly another day.

And I say to the ancient sky, "Arif was still young and knowing.
What was it to you if he should die another day?"

With whom did you have such strict transactions
The sheriff death could not wait to garnishee another day?

Had you some enmity with me or an argument with the sun,
Still you would stay to watch the children's glee another day.

By no means had the interval of sadness and happiness expired.
You're gone but you were meant to make do with me another day.

Only a fool asks me, "Ghalib why are you alive?"
My fate is to long for the day I will not be another day.

—translated from the Urdu by Andrew McCord

Ghazal

Archaeologist of feeling, would-be soothsayer of candor,
I work in the sun while I listen for thunder.

I see a coyote trot across a meadow slope, alert and calm,
like a mind for both a wild rose and a soaring condor.

Time that crawls over everything turns what is
to what was, and creates in us our sense of wonder.

We make love and unmake it, and we ask,
Why did she spurn him? Why did he wound her?

In summer, worshipped sunlight comes clear through green leaves
to praise the exploring ant whose only work is to wander.

In autumn, willow leaves migrate to the ground, the geese
fall southward, a letter homes to me marked "Return to Sender."

Some poplar that lives about as long as I will stand for me,
will wait in line as I write in lines, until we both go under.

If there comes a day when I can advance no further,
it's because on that day I have no father, no mother, no founder.

I slant through the wilderness, through the city of our common cause,
and all that is says, Reg, you must be persistent, undiscouraged, and tender.

Belief

Crouched beneath the Wailing Wall for my God,
I veil my eyes with a silver shawl for my God.

Like a gypsy gathering the folds of her skirt,
Penitent, to the damp earth I fall for my God.

Might this be Hell, eternal toil and confusion?
On my callused hands and knees I crawl. For my God

I push my faith like a wheelbarrow of mortar.
Why should I await Peter's roll call, for my God?

Like Michelangelo's melting Pieta,
In redemption's arms I sprawl for my God.

Sacrifice is a silent swan, preening her wings.
Words seem wasted, what's it all for? My God!

Yet belief weaves my voice in a great tapestry—
Heavenwards I nightly call for my God.

I brave Babel, Wordsworth's Bedouin wanderer,
Accepting whatever may befall for my God.

Miniature Ghazal

I thought of Kashmir today
And then remembered you today

Postcards yearning with evanescence—
Do you still wait for them today?

The blooded war, the season's calm,
Make storm-bred vigils for you today.

And yet your laughing verse moves on:
History can't hurt your soul today.

Ghalib, in 1858, said, Where is Delhi?
So too the absent place for you today.

You are your place. Your town. Your hills.
No giant negative is yours today.

The photographs of mailed-in memories
Make Sara post office for you today.

On Paradise

All those struggles to acquire Paradise,
then suddenly we're tired of Paradise.

For three years I made the drive, over an hour,
always turning at Brookshire, never Paradise.

He's the sad one, and the one most dangerous—
that old liar, ignorant of Paradise.

A small pond with a three-edged path around it—
So why, *why* are you looking for Paradise?

Money's on the table, ready for the bank.
Things aren't so dire, but almost like paradise.

My son, his lover—it's always a quarrel.
What's this heat, this desire, this paradise?

A '49 Merc with a milled flathead eight,
dangling from the keyring wire, a pair of dice.

Pacing in robes across green linoleum,
an anxious old friar, far from Paradise.

After months of looking, finally, a job.
Getting hired's a step closer to Paradise.

A garden surrounded by a mud brick wall,
smoke rising from a keeper's fire—Paradise.

Getting dressed, waiting for the mail, writing this,
have made JG tired. A nap. Ah. Paradise.

Ghazal

You say it's absurd—how could sunlight cause fevers?
In truth, you've surely seen moonlight cause fevers.

What shall I buy? This, That or the Other?
When admen's infernal delight cause fevers.

Van Gogh, Picasso, O'Keeffe understood:
Bathe your subject in light! Cause fevers.

What recompense? However I vote
Politicians' ambition and blight cause fevers.

Don't surrender. Take sustenance in knowing
the joy when poets' delight cause fevers.

Oh Shahid, you've treated me cruelly—such mad
intractable forms, when I write, cause fevers.

Ghazal on Half a Line by Adrienne Rich

In a familiar town, she waits for certain letters,
working out the confusion and the hurt in letters.

Whatever you didn't get—the job, the girl,
rejections are inevitably curt in letters.

This is a country with a post-office
where one can still make oneself heard in letters.

(Her one-street-over neighbor's Mme. de Sévigné
who almost always had the last word in letters.)

Was the disaster pendant from a tongue,
one she might have been able to avert in letters?

Still, acrimony, envy, lust, disdain
are land-mines the unconscious can insert in letters.

Sometimes more rage clings to a page than she would claim—
it's necessary to remain alert in letters

(as estranged friend donated to a library
three decades of her dishing out the dirt in letters)

and words which resonate and turn within
the mind can lie there flattened and inert in letters.

The tightest-laced precisely-spoken celibate
may inadvertently shrug off her shirt in letters.

Ex-lovers who won't lie down naked again
still permit themselves to flirt in letters.

What does Anonymous compose, unsigned
at night, after she draws the curtain? Letters.

The Red Dress of Poetry

After Jen mis-read the title of Seamus Heaney's "The Redress of Poetry"

Despite the lewd way you've eyed the red dress of poetry,
you've yet to get your heinie inside the red dress of poetry.

In days of old bards praised her lips, toes, tits in stilted prose.
Today? ACCESS DENIED behind the red dress of poetry.

Didja hear the one 'bout the salesman and the farmer's daughter?
He lost more than his pride beneath the red dress of poetry.

Shakespeare played a ghost, a servant: roles he could disappear in.
Yet he far preferred to hide in the red dress of poetry.

Baptist church girl finds her black tuxedoed groom at the altar,
vows next time she'll be a bride in the red dress of poetry.

Did Weldon Kees jump or did that rascal, Robinson, push him?
All we're sure of is he died in the red dress of poetry.

Though highland gents are fond of brisk, tickling breeze on their balls,
I reckon their hips too wide for the red dress of poetry.

A war ain't really a war til a few young 'uns get napalmed;
It's no prom til someone's cried on the red dress of poetry.

While gray Nobels and stately Laureates limp out to pasture,
a young jockey spurs the side of The Red Dress of Poetry.

If Seamus Heaney appeared in drag on the back of the book,
I can assure you I would read: *"The Redress of Poetry."*

The shamus, case closed, scowls down on his city's lascivious skin.
Daniel's cuffed, takes a down-town ride in the red dress of poetry.

Souvenir

He gazed into the air, searching for a word in my language.
I blinked. Across the pool a zephyr stirred, in my language.

Where was I? Where was he? Where he looked, remembering?
The air was his release; his burden, my language.

Our silence was the air itself, and the moment timeless
(though a timeless moment is absurd, in my language).

So it would always be with us, back and forth:
what he implied in his, I inferred in my language.

Plain speech? There's no such thing! I can't tell you
how much the overwrought can undergird in my language.

Did he clear his throat? Did rain fall? Can there really be
a ringing bell or a singing bird in my language?

He blurted out the word in his own tongue, like a bell rung,
a distant bell, whose very speech was slurred, in my language.

Who am I now, gone crystalline with waiting, listening
for what I still have never heard in my language?

Ghazal

Trying to fly in the meantime
ready to dry in the meantime

flocks of turds have fun with words
wanting to rely in the meantime

herds of sheep don't love you as I do
waiting to tie in the meantime

licorice love intoxicates trees
about to expire and die in the meantime

obsessed with masturbation and desiring sex
teens begin to cry in the meantime

depending upon the density of fat
pigs float by in the meantime

For the Man in the Yellow Leather Jacket

A window translates out of absence in the night.
His body passed—a simple tense—in the night.

Open, a foreign blizzard entered the room.
Twice he woke, missing her presence in the night.

He thought in fragments, shards of colored glass.
Only the ear makes sense in the night.

Siberia was a white dream, a worn salt lick of stars.
Who has not offered their innocence in the night?

He felt it slip through the seams of yellow leather.
The Black Sea is its own iridescence in the night.

Wind a cold horseshoe, held against the skin.
He made, from its history, a present tense in the night.

Footsteps across frozen grass call out your name.
Mandelstam, your eyes still press into the night.

Calamity, Angel

They've splayed his wings, disinterred this angel,
certain to have overheard this angel.

Infect the leaves with heaven's fever—
a crown of flames has blurred this angel.

Tonight black teeth grind lime;
he flaps and crows, a filthy bird, this angel.

His feet are bound, his lips sewn shut;
Sear with torch and cross, gird this angel.

He slurs your name; dim threads unwind—
they have frankincensed and myrrhed this angel.

Take this silver, this knot of garlic;
we burn to forget, to reword this angel.

James, your hands are stunted, your breath cold—
listen to me: surely you've murdered this angel.

Spring Wedding

for Laura and Bernard (April 12, 1998)

Such bold spirits: birds sally in spring
calling "Hear me, hear me" in spring.

Sunlight through chartreuse leaves
shimmers on the lonely in spring.

Are we prone to secrets? accidents? love?
An owl feather drifts through cherry in spring.

A wasp lands among pine needles, hops, zooms
to a twig, rubbing its wings, hungry in spring.

Ruminant in the woods, a poet (beckoning insight)
blinks her third eye (the better to see in spring!)

Cathedral bells chime through the town square,
ringing good news from the belfry in spring.

Bernard and Laura, dashing lovers wed in a gala
Easter's fete, savor their luxury in spring.

Here we are at last! they cry,
two gracing fidelity in spring.

The pastor's blessing wafts among us,
his syntax scented by the calla lily in spring.

We, too, once in love, rolled through myrtle,
purple lupin, and the piquant daisy in spring.

We thought life an inexhaustible wealth,
so limitless, an eternity, in spring.

Now we pose for pictures, sing of rain in Spain and—
inebriates of hope—toast until tipsy in spring.

Why bother the wise? Banish
pain with this plenty in spring!

Ghazal on Ghazals

For couplets the ghazal is prime; at the end
Of each one's a refrain like a chime: "*at the end.*"

But in subsequent couplets throughout the whole poem,
It's this second line only will rhyme at the end.

On a string of such strange, unpronounceable fruits,
How fine the familiar old lime at the end!

All our writing is silent, the dance of the hand,
So that what it comes down to's all mime, at the end.

Dust and ashes? How dainty and dry! We decay
To our messy primordial slime at the end.

Two frail arms of your delicate form I pursue,
Inaccessible, vibrant, sublime at the end.

You gathered all manner of flowers all day,
But your hands were most fragrant of thyme, at the end.

There are so many sounds! A poem having one rhyme?
—A good life with a sad, minor crime at the end.

Each new couplet's a different ascent: no great peak,
But a low hill quite easy to climb at the end.

Two armed bandits: start out with a great wad of green
Thoughts, but you're left with a dime at the end.

Each assertion's a knot which must shorten, alas,
This long-worded rope of which I'm at the end.

Now Qafia Radif has grown weary, like life,
At the game he's been wasting his time at. THE END.

Ghazal: The Shade of the Author of Indian Love Lyrics Speaks

Less than the dust beneath (O hear her plea tonight!)
Thy chariot wheel, is one of low degree tonight.

Less than the weed that grows beside thy door
Even less am I, smaller yet than wee tonight.

Less than the rust that—never mind the rest:
All the tarnished similes agree tonight.

Imprisoned in pre-post-colonial drivel
How shall embracing darkness set me free tonight?

Through the dark courtyard, shall I silently
Make my escape when you get up to pee tonight?

Cut loose now from its mooring my sad dhow,
Shall I let it drift westward from your quay tonight?

I, whose submissive silence hid my heart,
Laugh and sing like the Miller of the Dee tonight

The fountain plashes and the bulbul trills
(I shall go mad if I don't get some zee tonight)

Alas, my lonely cup is cold and dry
No longer tea for two and two for tea tonight

A mightier ruler soon shall have me, his
All-conquering hand shall yet caress my knee tonight.

I welcome him. Farewell, Zahiruddin:
I beg no crumb, I make no final plea tonight

To make it keen and bright, behold how I
Take here thy sword and grease it up with ghee tonight.

Poor hopeless Laurence! Now, Love's last reward,
Death comes for Mrs. Nicholson (that's me) tonight.

For Marthe

I give homage to my mother, the image of my mother,
the edge of her solemn words, the fine carriage of my mother.

The hive exhales the swarm, a barrage of dust against the sun.
What is empty dies out, an unused language to a mother.

A concoction of clouds, fallen and moon-ridged on the river.
So it was written on the unread page of my mother.

Conception in a hidden pod—sages speak of birth and death.
Moonlit gauze of lunar moths over bones that cage our mothers.

One season glides, blue ice, another rages with fire and wind.
To keep their secrets from us asked for courage from our mothers.

Larvae tremble on a shadowy stage of the still forest.
We are destined to suffer was the badge of my mother.

For Colette, it occurred—wages of beauty and light accrued.
With these *ahas* arrived a fragile knowledge of her mother.

Four Ghazals

I.

Once I get walking, I could walk for miles, this mild night.
What keeps me caught in the net of tears & smiles, this mild night?

See how every car has headlights to reveal the hidden road?
Leafing through my heart, what dark this head compiles, this mild night.

We go & listen to the words; then we disperse. It's never-ending.
May one enter a poetry knowing no exiles, this mild night?

Again the moon is waxing. Immaculate lunacies loom.
Spool out the oldest yarn: it still beguiles, this mild night.

Have you noticed how the lights exhibit red & green forever?
Ardeo! this rolling sea reveals no isles, this mild night.

II.

It's a dangerous business, wandering into the lane of poetry.
First there's dazzlement; then: surprise! The pain of poetry.

I kept on passing this vacant alley, thinking I'd find some enterprise!
Each time, I lost something else. My loss was the gain of poetry.

Everyone thinks they know what house she lives in. Does she sleep
in this bed or this bed? Why don't you ask the disdain of poetry?

Not to paint a bleak picture: One smile—no, even
a chance hint of her gentle smile—becomes the precious chain of poetry.

What's this prattle, Ardeo? There's no subject, just some anarchistic
                                             hillside.
I can feel a dark cloud—though not yet the royal rain of poetry.

III.

We're rapping on the door of conditional existence. Who will answer?
I've got everything in my knapsack—anguish, wit, persistence—but no
answer.

We came to this far outpost because they'd announced a party.
Now they wheel around corpses. For this distance, who will answer?

I don't really care if it's warm or cold; I know it always changes.
All I want now is a lively fight. I'm the resistance—if you're the answer.

I'm going to get into the dailiness game, just like everyone else.
Even the sun & moon have enlisted! At every instance, there's a different
answer.

Listen, Ardeo! You don't know what you're talking about; you're full of
shit.
Isn't it weird when even ordure cries, with insistence, for a rosy answer?

IV.

Every failure was perhaps a disguise for some other thing.
If I can't discern what, I lack the eyes for some other thing.

The forgiveness that sustains me now is like high-proof moonshine:
for each stupidity, another swig. This makes me wise to some other thing.

No, this is not the place for excuses; did you try the shop down the road?
We ran out long ago. All we've got are supplies for some other thing.

Maybe—maybe I can start everything over again from scratch.
Syllables?—present; ideas?—yeah, got some. Now stir in sighs for some
other thing.

Whenever you play with words, we always wind up confused, Ardeo!
Do you take us for a wind-up toy? Or would you surmise we're some
other thing?

By Your Nature

Who questions your truth, hypnotized by your nature:
Enticed with a bris, circumcised by your nature?

Our hunters all covered with musk and menstruation
mask their confusion, now disguised by your nature.

The last oracle sleeps with a scarab in his hand.
A cruel prophecy exercised by your nature.

Shamefully, they flee from the frailty of their city,
through brackish remains yet crystallized by your nature.

Stone now my tablet, such poor penmanship: Dear M.
(circa Exodus) *"I wasn't surprised by your nature."*

. . . no longer a science, what now, only hope?
When ambiguity is all we've surmised by your nature.

Under darkling scud, the desert exhales her final plea:
"James, just go; don't be compromised by your nature!"

An Introductory Ghazal

"This is an invitation" are the words of my brother.
After all, as a poet, isn't Hafiz my brother?

I enter the garden, his scent still trapped in sweat
Beaded pale on the face of the briar-rose, my brother.

An example of overkill: in this sugar-coated world
When a child I stole Dum-Dums and Pez from my brother.

My lover waits outside, his heavy breath is sweet.
Why can't I kiss him—who says he's my brother?

Oh, the world is vain. But then, so am I.
Look muse, I'll be blunt. Simon-says, be my brother.

Now as Zaynab the eager goes in search of the rose
First to you, kind *agha*, says *Khoda hafiz*, my brother.

Ghazal

Shards of conscience cut me, though never in time.
I always act wicked in space, yet never in time.

Look, words descend on us like angels,
But to wrestle them, we must be clever in time.

Do I loom over others or do they loom over me?
Living here, I'd feel like Gulliver in time.

Ah, the poet's mirrored paradise—
Fame, and our music beating forever in time.

Our days are tied to boulders rolling downhill.
So, roll faster! By God, push the lever in, Time!

My body, a rosebud; his a wandering bee.
We will fade—will he ever endeavor in time?

Between bowls of desire and guilt I sit—
Oh Zaynab, just gulp down whatever in time!

Poland Ghazal

Two stubborn names she must remember to forget
In case she's ever detained they have sworn her to forget

Adoring students crowd her feet and grin
A witness from overseas in the series Never To Forget

Whose bed am I headed for which night is this
This November will take all of December to forget

What was it on the list was it oranges or Brillo
I don't set my mind to forgetting it's either remember or forget

Snowflakes tick the windshield night empties out its tacks
Imagine how exactly one would *labor* to forget

The tremor in her voice pitched to thrill our little gasps
Hard enough to forgive even harder to forget

The dire song of the century ringing in our ears
Promise always to remember before you remember to forget

Ghazal

April's anenomes are finally coming back
In May nothing's final the season of comebacks

Michael Jordan has returned though his father hasn't
Always the finalist forget *I'm never coming back*

To reach a certain age more behind than lies ahead
The more finality looms the more the vivid hours come back

What I love about verse is how it veers and delays
Before the final right margin then deftly comes back

Mother dead for thirty years I've been dreaming all night long
Must finish my final in Religion true or false she's coming back

O scissor-tail swallows warm all winter in Brazil
Inner gates so wide open what final brainstorm shrieked come back

A millennium is closing here's champagne to all my friends
With its murderous finale who would welcome it back

God's sitting this one out just as He has the rest
In the all-but-final analysis He never intended to come back

The poet's taped voice from beyond death itself
Fills the chapel with his whole being as the final words come back

And back to haunt me because what are we but voice
Amazed final bodies that are never coming back

The Life Story of Eddie "Son House" James, Jr. as Told Through His Hands

In the fields, she touched me with dew-moist hands.
She was the earth lifted in my blue hands.

A man must live to have a life to sing.
He dies to have ashes lifted by hands.

Are there no limits to a bluesman's life?
Cotton & guitars: Picked by the same hands.

A train's whistle holds possibilities
Much like the backsides or the palms of hands.

In the audience, there are more blue eyes
Than I recall my hometown had black hands.

If you think these are wrinkles in my face,
Come, hear my life story told through my hands.

A preacher is nothing but a bluesman.
Bible? Guitar? All the same in my hands.

A workday is so long; the hours immense.
But my grip! Look at the size of these hands.

Your spirit becomes your eyes in prison.
Who questions a spirit with two strong hands?

Evie, with workdays as large as your eyes,
No one strums blues from my bones like your hands.

Ghazal

A single telephone rings starts a sleepless hour.
Shattering the silent night, it prolongs the hour.

The stars smirk at your bad posture. Haunt you.
Haunt the sweaty white sheets during the long hour.

You like to share the distant news with your lover.
He is lost in his dream world during the long hour.

You chant and take deep breaths to keep your cool.
Still, the moment is prolonged into an unending hour.

Some memories cast deep shadows on the walls.
Like echoes, they can't move your hopeless hour.

Go ahead, imagine a herd of sheep on the ceiling.
Count them; it might save you from a boring hour.

The dawn pours rainbows on the windowpanes.
Weary, you feel the passing of an endless hour.

You see the shapes moving in the sun, changing.
You know, you have survived the nasty, night hour.

A friend asks about the dark rings around your eyes.
Only then you moan, groaning about the sleepless hour.

Perhaps the nightmare will continue into a daydream,
But Bhagwan will not feel the pain of your long hour.

A Dream World

How long will you be lost in a dream world?
You imagine everything green of the dream world.

You sang while the sky changed colors. Alas!
Your lover never cared to share your dream world.

The stars came to guide you in the wind's direction.
But the blinking fireflies confused your dream world.

You went to paint a sunrise. A cloud mystified you.
Took your breath away in a mysterious dream world.

Soaking in rain, you ran for a dry spot in the rainbow.
Did you ever come close to it in your dream world?

When the fall will come, you'll shiver like a dry leaf.
You'll imagine the spring colors of the dream world.

Life is full of memories, full of fallen flowers, leaves.
It's a bag full of mulching colors of the lost world.

Dive within. Search your Self. Don't get caught.
These are the fake flowers of the dream world.

O Bhagwan, smell the tea leaves! Don't jump.
Get off the bridge and cross over to the real world.

In Another Country

In Kashmir, half asleep, Mother listens to the rain.
In Manhattan, I feel her presence in the rain.

A rooster precedes the Call to Prayer at Dawn:
God is a name-dropper: all names at once in the rain.

Forsythia shrivel in a glass vase on her nightstand
On my window sills, wilted petals, petulance in the rain.

She must wonder when he will put on the kettle
butter the crumpets, offer compliments to the rain.

She yawns, performs ablutions, across the oceans
water in my hands becomes a reverence in the rain.

At Jewel House in Srinagar, Mother reshapes my ghazal,
"No enjambments!" she says. "Wah, Wah," I chant in the rain.

"Rafiq," I hear her call over the city din
The kettle whistles: my mother's scent in the rain.

Your Name

I live by the shine of this candle, your name.
I live in the echo of this canto, your name.

Crazy tree in a throttle of wind abrades the slate sky;
Breath similarly, under buttons. All frictions kindle your name.

Good road hum. My coffee on the dashboard's traced
against the sky, in steam, a little contrail: your name.

Like other men, I listen: *time*. I know no hour's
chime bell but whose toll can tell your name.

Archaic riddle: what song a world without
(If such could be) could sure be reckoned Hell? Your name.

Ghazal

The first time I saw you I—but that's not strictly true, love.
And that's nothing either to do with the nature of rue, love.

What the French call *frisson*, what the wind breathes *shiver*,
What confuses the skin of the spine, what the Scots call *grue*, love . . .

Wave-chuck, goose-honk, scrape of the wind's kimono, moon-hiss:
It's all in a lung. Listen up: I'll bark till I mew, love!

Always backwards, us (except those goings to Paris)
Correct? Let's wish back the clock: let's say *la la oo*, love.

Dunkirk, Culloden, Maginot, Agincourt, Rubicon.
Dunkirk, Passchendaele, yesterday, Waterloo, love.

Ink dries slowly on expensive paper. How the grave howls.
I try to think of poetry again. I think you'll find a new love.

First *thee! Thee only, only, only, only, only!*
Then later this, in blood: *Just you, but you, love.*

Six continents, a land of Nod, an *nth* dimension.
Whoever mentioned elsewhere? Where were you? I never knew, love.

The last time—could that be?—the hearts' blood hammering . . .
Him. Not my home. Not a bedroom's whom's who, love.

What's a marriage without rage and murmur and rummaging doctors
Who've a wrench, as the saying goes, for every screw, love?

____*of my life*____*of my life*____*of my life*____*of my life*
Fill in the blank. That's the coop you flew, love.

The high hayrick sways under thunder and fat rain drops.
Summer's over. Find cover? O what in the world are we going to do, love?

Do thee I worse Richard richer take take forsaking for . . .
Better close the book. God's word, it wasn't true love.

Miscellany

Spread the tarot with care with me.
Future is daily fare with me.

Cats know eyeing can unnerve.
If you agree, come stare with me.

A confidence is heading here,
a dangerous need to share with me.

An Anjou lost no one an Eden.
Regard the innocent pear with me.

Hounds are privileged and many.
I choose to hide the hare with me.

Remorse outruns us every time—
A daily loss to bear with me.

He loses hold. The tugging globe
lifts to upper air with me.

A King has little power, it's clear.
Leave what you have to spare with me.

Ghazal

G begins the last name of two pianists I love:
Gould's voice, I hear; Goode, in one week see thrice—Christ, I love!

An old folded lady like Mother, I said I'd not
be, and wasn't (and am); she too heard, "Your breasts, I love."

A poet now, I don't dream my dead babies are red-
haired little boys, smiling, in smocks—what exists, I love.

There the father was, eating lettuce, not speaking, his
uncouth buxom girlfriend crimping the pie crust I love.

The nursery lady raises chicks like the teacher's
aide whose diverted (she nurses hedgehogs) lusts I love.

I keep ex's tree, never liked maiden Orgel: what
it meant (found in Bach); how it sounded—Bach's *kunst*, I love.

On the Table

I was taught to smooth the aura at the end
said my masseuse, hands hovering at the end.

Inches above my placid pummeled self
did I feel something floating at the end?

Is my naked body merely prone
to ectoplasmic vapors to no end?

Many another arthritic has lain here
seeking to roll pain's ball end over end.

Herbal oils, a CD playing soft
loon calls, wave laps, bird trills now must end.

I rise and dress, restored to lift and bend,
my ethereal wisp invisible at the end.

Ghazal

We tried all night to see it, that last star falling,
Even with help, it was a close but no cigar falling.

No one speaks so clearly about paper hats adrift at sea.
In the spray is only another oceanic grammar falling.

The statue of noseless grandmothers rises without a hitch.
What could we say: better that than of the czar falling.

Few children spare a dime on streets of broken records,
Without a song, the only note from the scimitar falling.

Our Beloved has left the building; everything is unrevokable.
The peace and quiet are dead, the near and far falling.

A telephoto lens chases us to Reno, steals our laundry,
Heedless of dignity and faster than a film star falling.

Our hair has thickened since, our clothes just thin paper:
this hurricane, we are in a shower of rose attar falling.

Weaning us is difficult off that teat that doesn't flag.
Confronted by luminousness, who notices a milk jar falling?

My name, Hunger, is Anthony. Remember me, my traveler.
None will remember from what cloud you and I are falling.

Faintly

Does the house settle   then rust faintly
or is it raining or   rain just faintly

His finger pointed for   the world a tiny bird
perched then vanishing   as it must faintly

Fear stays and carries   her to a cradled bed
a tide reveals itself   begins to adjust faintly

Do nothing till you   hear how much I can bear
In my good ear just   speak of lust faintly

The Beloved cannot go   so quickly as yet
See we traced your name   in the dust faintly

Treasonous routes back   alley songs and murders
Friend forget everything   we discussed faintly

A cottage reminds good   fortune it's homespun
Its industry from days   yes of august faintly

Smoke rises from graves   Anthony dug and divided
in worlds where fruits   stars organs combust faintly

Cursed Philosophy, The Destruction of the Philosophers

Go liars! You've earned your first "second naïveté."
Your thoughts stir complex, rehearsed second naïveté.

Fucking hypocrites! Keepers of the hierarchies.
You wander in an accursed second naïveté.

Look at the concatenation of filth upon filth!
Its *Ghusl* is interspersed second naïveté.

God has abandoned you in Babylon forever.
Wander that land with a thirst—second naïveté.

Economics steers the ordeal of civility.
Civilization: coerced second naïveté!

Of course, it tests your powers of renunciation.
Later, you get reimbursed second naïveté.

Hold yourself together and try not to fall apart!
Hold fast the core, the dispersed second naïveté.

Naïveté: dialectical ontology.
Dialogue: strangely conversed second naïveté.

Knowledge forms the morass of your dogmatic substrate.
You teach those with a well-versed second naïveté.

The thoughts you think with are traversed this way and that way.
Weird geometry: transversed second naïveté.

If only Ibn Rushd (Averroes) were still alive!
Then metaphysics would burst second naïveté.

But you are lost. In your blind interpretations drowned.
Love of wisdom—in immersed second naïveté.

And Sophia does not love you, nor God, nor Satan.
Like *Domini Cannes*—worst second naïveté.

Destiny Haunts

Love's drunkard shines this scimitar for you.
Rough swoons will pierce a stranger in a bar—for you.

To paradise, the needle's eye is shut—
a camel kneels in purgatory's tar for you.

Nevermind hatching fish, swims upstream.
The soggy world will turn to caviar for you.

No, listen! It's caught, I tell you, now—
passing hand to hand at the bazaar for you.

Petrified, the trees uproot and drain.
Elixirs concoct phantoms in that jar for you.

Young heart, your boasting crucifies my ear.
Hush—an arrow rides desire's frantic scar for you.

A pipe is not a pipe nor sign a sign—
So what! My secret stash keeps a cigar for you!

That day, the horizon cracked, let her through.
Her note—"The future, the past's avatar—For You."

Shahid, you see these prospects do me in.
Whisper, "Kelly, even this, my yaar, for you."

Ghazal

Each syllable unwinds its shy request in time.
Speak slowly, show me what it means to rest in time.

Eyes lit from above, untouched chambers, clues to what?
A boy's photograph (*Do I love him?*) pressed in time.

Link kiss to wound, pluck to string and page to turn:
your wrinkled face will pass the cherub's test in time.

I know the type—scented, moneyed, everything tucked.
For him, the fraying sleeves we all get dressed in: Time.

Give me something. What? I don't know. A decent pen.
I'll shake (scrape?) something off my tongue (the pest!) in time.

All I have: memory's long afterburn, and you—
my blanketed cargo, my small craft, blessed in time.

Whole nights run as fingers, counting out the palm;
hands pressed beneath what passes unexpressed in time.

The forgotten portion, plain and tough, what to do?
Steep it, she said, her voice the quietest, *in thyme*.

My dark strokes wrestle moonlight until the room sways;
heartless ink, bring me sweet dreams, unstressed, stressed, in time.

The dead say nothing but what lingers, left undone.
Cold fate to say he'd climb Mt. Everest in time.

So, Kelly's really gone? Does anyone know where?
Third hand, I heard it said she would go West, in time.

I Am a Ghazal

How many souls can I amass in my hands?
Caught, will they melt to a morass in my hands?

I open like a lily to the April morning sky:
The sun paints its cups of molten brass in my hands.

I am Genghis! I shall crush the golden lands that extend
from Herat to the frigid Khyber Pass in my hands!

I clutch the whirling Earth—the clouds lean down like gods,
drenching the sweet, rough grass in my hands.

I am Gaia—and the spirits of the glowworms, screech owls, rhinos,

                                        mosses,
and grandiose sequoias are—Alas!—in my hands.

By torchlight in Lucifer's crystal-walled den,
I'm amazed to find clots of rubasse in my hands.

I am Gaby. Nightmares, poems, and my aching, aging head
are ghost-ships of fleecy-spun glass in my hands.

Dark Ghazal

As if in a sea's starlight-edging dark,
I floated in the moonlight, and the dark.

Prim puddles of moon, calipers of cold,
I was St. Brendan in an age called "Dark."

Black ice made my Subaru spin starboard,
My car afloat off Waldo in the dark.

Funny how life slows, even seems to halt,
Sludged fast in fields beyond the blacktop's dark.

I thought my heart had lost its beat and drift,
Like a stream where sunlight leaves stems of dark.

Once, uncandled, flashlight lost, power out,
I scribbled poems on walls to fight the dark.

No TV, I turned to you, tried to talk,
Cold shouldered by love in a house of dark.

For what machine could help me bite my tongue
Once I've hurt you saying things filled with dark?

Scraped down past thought, out the door, Stuart stumbled,
Dogged, hunted, by proximities, of dark.

Drink, My Love, and Deeply

The alakazam surprise in this world:
Love's miracle never dies in this world.

Amphibious mortals straddle earth and sky:
Origins we improvise in this world.

Alchemy succeeds at pouring light from stone,
Creates fantasy without lies in this world.

Rainbows at your temples lead me to willing
Splendor in your eyes: my prize in this world.

Fingers on your shoulders easing out the wings
Coax your drowsing dream to arise in this world.

When it's clear a simple kiss will change your life
Trust the liquid sunrise in this world.

In sublime seductive cadence, strangers
Harmonize a little reprise in this world.

Dazzle

I need some kind of talisman or charm
to protect those I love from my drear charm.

"Regret is the fruit of pity," grumbled
Genghis Khan, fingering a good luck charm.

Parkas, guns, trap-lines and ice-fishing. Who
wouldn't turn her head to surprise some charm?

He blushed. He fumbled in his lap and at
his feet. Dear God help him find his lost charm.

If it's not under pressure, it's not grace,
but only manners. Or, even worse, charm.

Frazzle

All for one and one for all was our motto after all
our tribulations. And then we'd each go home, after all.

By the people. For the people. Of the people. Grammar—
but politics is an incomplete sentence, after all.

"Better to have loved and lost . . . ," the poet wrote.
Than to have won? Poetry dotes on loss, after all.

They don't take the flag down at dusk, the patriot grumbled.
A country's too big to love, but not a rule, after all.

How would you translate "self service" or "lube job"
if you had a dirty mind and scant English, after all?

Veil (bee-keeper's? bridal?), Vale (tears), Vail (Colorado).
Phonics? No avail. Better learn to spell, after all.

The love of repetition is the root of all form?
Well, liturgy and nonsense are cousins, after all.

"I cannot tell a lie," he said, which was a lie,
but not the kind for which the bill comes after all.

Guzzle

I need a loan. I need a drink. I need
not to be perceived to be in need.

You must change your life, scolds Rilke.
Just how big a diaper will I need?

There's skill and merit and, of course, good looks,
and charm, and nepotism. Also, need.

Ant to grasshopper: How about some bread?
Grasshopper to ant: Whatever you knead.

Death and taxes. Dearth and taxis. Breath, stealth,
lies and faxes. 1-800-EYE-NEED.

Gifts, courtesies, surprises like grenades—
let them supplant this prattle about need.

Muzzle

Some people like the idea of silence.
Let them try the drab thing itself: silence.

A cat stalking a roach, ears up, belly
dusting the floor—a statue of silence.

The child balks. Why? It says only, "Because."
The adult equivalent is silence.

The city never sleeps? How wrong you are.
Douse, snuff, *basta*, fuck off, sleep tight. Silence.

God breathed over the waters, and they begat
their swells and troughs. Well then, what is silence?

Put your tongue into it, it stains your tongue
black as a parrot's whose name is "Silence."

OK, Mr. Know-It-All, let's compromise.
Tell all but translate it into silence.

A tree falls where no human hears it crash;
do its siblings mourn for it in silence?

Puzzle

What's her allure? Her wan smile? Her figure?
Love's not blind, but myopic. Go figure.

The house is haunted. *Oh, by whom?* By you.
Damn. Am I an absence or a figure?

He entered the room drenched in humdrum,
like an accountant recording a figure.

There's never one thing you don't know that holds
you back—a password, sure thing or a figure.

Let's couple. Let's multiply. If we then
divide, the lawyers will set a figure.

Drizzle

Baudelaire: "The dead, the poor dead, have their bad hours."
But the dead have no watches, no grief and no hours.

At first not smoking took all my time: I did it
a little by little and hour by hour.

Per diem. Pro bono. Cui bono? Pro rata.
But the poor use English. *Off and on. By the hour.*

"I'm sorry but we'll have to stop now." There tick but
fifty minutes in the psychoanalytic hour.

Vengeance is mine, yours, his or hers, ours, yours again
(you-all's this time), and then (yikes!) theirs. I prefer ours.

Twenty minutes fleeing phantoms at full tilt and then
the cat coils herself like a quoit and sleeps for hours.

Nozzle

A thousand and three in Italy alone. . . .
He can't leave women or himself alone.

The title of that Christmas's hit movie
seemed to me redundant: *Home Alone*.

The narrow street of sleep opens into
populous dreams, and then one wakes alone.

My eyes, balls, nostrils and hands come in pairs;
the mouth, navel and penis are alone.

For all the bluster about needing space,
it's claustrophobic living alone.

Bad company, my parents called my friends.
But what name did they have for me alone?

Ghazal

So many leaves are falling that it's clear to me
Last night they grew a wood and towed it near to me.

There aren't so many leaves as are arriving there,
Like friends of mine—I've fewer than are dear to me.

The leaves were on the tree, the lane and everywhere,
Save any clearing where they now appear to me.

All year a tree that had to pose for poetry
Was waiting, now it plays the balladeer to me!

It casts the verses in its head then carelessly
Unlooses them, a whirl of a career to me.

When the wind rests the leaves are high or fallen low:
I close my eyes and something smells of fear to me;

Then it harasses them from where they had to go,
Suggests they try to fly and some fly here to me.

This jumbling progress home that's all there is to them
Is the profoundest trice of the whole year to me;

Elsewhere the evergreens are darkened all the same,
Their stressful lamentations insincere to me.

One leaf the leaves adore and follow into space
Is buried in what's nothing but a smear to me,

But one they think abandoned in their sudden race
Rides down alone, and that will bring some cheer to me.

For here's one of its kind from the old Celtic tree:
By winter may the ground have lent an ear to me.

After Magritte

The sill is clammy to the touch, and the view familiar.
But doesn't that moon seem a little *too* familiar?

His severed hand had been in someone's pocket.
The stars hang perilously above Rue Familiar.

The whore's pigeons seemed safe under his bowler,
But when he spotted an opening, the banker grew familiar.

His cloud saddle strapped to the sky's flanks,
The Liberator arrived out of the blue. Familiar

Ideas, like glass shards, lay all over the floor,
Each with a part of the field pasted to familiar

Problems from the front page—the war, the scandals.
Men in uniform left us free to pursue familiar

Desires: But which came first, the cage or the egg?
What you dreamt was overdue, what you knew familiar.

Who owns the light? Who sold the sea and its waves?
Perspective is the devil's new familiar.

If all property is theft, nothing is left to give
The old man in Brussels but a few familiar

Imitations on cheap posters, enough to make seem
Strange what delicacies had been hitherto familiar.

Here is the pearl that made a grain of sand,
And the bricked-up alphabet that made you familiar.

Ghazal of the Better-Unbegin

Too volatile, am I? too voluble? too much a word-person?
I blame the soup: I'm a primordially stirred person.

Two pronouns and a vehicle was Icarus with wings.
The apparatus of his selves made an absurd person.

The animals are naked, but one hides a worse intent.
In your menagerie, who's feathered? who's the furred person?

The noise I make is sympathy's: sad dogs are tied afar.
But (howling) I become the ever more unheard person.

There's insufficient peace in numbers, ghostwriting the book.
Two dads per Jesus is the limit (and one bird per son).

I need a hundred more of you to make a likelihood.
The mirror's not convincing—that at-best inferred person.

As time's revealing gets revolting, I start looking out.
Look in and what you see is one unholy blurred person.

The only cure for birth one doesn't love to contemplate.
Better to be an unsung song, an unoccurred person.

Heather, you'll be the death of me—each fifth and second studied!
Addressing you this way, I make us our own third person.

Harm's Way

How did someone come at last to the word for patience
and know that it was the right word or patience

the sounds had come such a distance from the will to give pain
which that person kept like a word for patience

the word came on in its own time like a star
at such a distance from either pain or patience

it echoed someone in a mirror who threatened with fire
an immortal with no bounds of hatred or patience

the syllables were uttered out of the sound of fire
but in silence they became the word for patience

it is not what the hawk hangs on or the hushed fox
waits with who do not need a word for patience

passing through the sound of another's pain
it brings with it something of that pain or patience

but how did whoever first came to it convey
to anyone else that it was the word for patience

they must have arrived at other words by then
to be able to use something from pain for patience

there is no such word in the ages of the leaves
in the days of the grass there is no name for patience

many must have traveled the whole way without knowing
that what they wanted was the word for patience

it is as far from patience as William is from me
and yet known to be patience the word for patience

The Causeway

This is the bridge where at dusk they hear voices
far out in the meres and marshes or they say they hear voices

the bridge shakes and no one else is crossing at this hour
somewhere along here is where they hear voices

this is the only bridge though it keeps changing
from which some say they always hear voices

the sounds pronounce an older utterance out of the shadows
sometimes stifled sometimes carried from clear voices

what can be recognized in the archaic syllables
frightens many and tells others not to fear voices

travellers crossing the bridge have forgotten where they were going
in a passage between the remote and the near voices

there is a tale by now of a bridge a long time before this one
already old before the speech of our day and the mere voices

when the Goths were leaving their last kingdom in Scythia
they could feel the bridge shaking under their voices

the bank and the first spans are soon lost to sight
there seemed no end to the horses carts people and all their voices

in the mists at dusk the whole bridge sank under them
into the meres and marshes leaving nothing but their voices

they are still speaking the language of their last kingdom
that no one remembers who now hears their voices

whatever translates from those rags of sound
persuades some who hear them that they are familiar voices

grandparents never seen ancestors in their childhoods
now along the present bridge they sound like dear voices

some may have spoken in my own name in an earlier language
when last they drew breath in the kingdom of their voices

Ghazal

Men must age into your shape for I see you everywhere.
Trace of a trace—ephemeral—but like dew everywhere.

Long dead, yet living in all men I see,
Like desire, you were, I knew everywhere.

Come, come with me to a place beyond belief—
I know you live, you man of gold, untrue everywhere.

Arms enwrap darkness, bracelets circle the bone.
Lost fullness of myth but its residue everywhere.

Some of us nomads who wander uncommitted
with borrowed belonging imagine Xanadu everywhere.

The Little Black Book

It was Aisling who first soft-talked my penis-tip between her legs
while teasing open that velcro-strip between her legs.

Cliona, then. A skinny country girl.
The small stream, in which I would skinny-dip, between her legs.

Born and bread in Londinium, the standoffish Etain,
who kept a stiff upper lip between her legs.

Grainne. Grain-goddess. The last, triangular shock of corn,
through which a sickle might rip, between her legs.

Again and again that winter I made a bee-line for Ita,
for the sugar-water sip between her legs.

The spring brought not only Liadan but her memory of Cuirithir,
his ghostly oneupmanship between her legs.

(Ita is not to be confused with her steely half-sister, Niamh,
she of the ferruginous drip between her legs.)

It was Niamh, as luck would have it, who introduced me to Orla.
The lost weekend of a day-trip between *her* legs.

It was Orla, as luck would have it, who introduced me to Roisin.
The bramble-patch. The rosehip between her legs.

What ever became of Sile?
Sile who led me to horse-worship between her legs.

As for Janet from the Shankill, who sometimes went by "Sinead,"
I practised my double back-flip between her legs.

I had a one-on-one tutorial with Siobhan.
I first heard of *The Singapore Grip* between her legs.

And what ever became of Sorcha, Sorcha, Sorcha?
Her weakness for the whip between her legs.

Or the big-boned, broad-shouldered Treasa?
She asked me to give her a buzzclip between her legs.

Or the little black sheep, Una, who kept her own little black book?
I fluttered, like an erratum-slip, between her legs.

A Double Ghazal for Seamus Heaney

I shall say no more about Lough Derg, only that it is reported that 7,000 pilgrims
visit it every year during the Station season, which lasts from the 1st of June to
the 15th of August, that Muldoon the ferryman pays the landlord 150 pounds per
annum . . .

—John O'Donovan, from a letter of November 1st, 1835

New York. November. The Pierpont Morgan's or the Frick's sky high
chandeliers. Tuxes. Dicky-bows. Low-cut silks and cambrics, sky high

satins and cuttanees. Canapés. Cabernet, albeit *Sutter Home*, and "dry"
white wine. Then, "You're home," a familiar voice mutters, "home and dry."

A crowd-hush. You're togged out still, but in a football jersey.
Limbering up to send one of your famous free kicks sky high.

You're sixteen, the age I was when, at Armagh Museum,
I was held up to you by Jerry Hicks, held by Hicks sky high.

The crowd-hush. The goal-posts freshly painted green, white and gold.
The cattle driven into the next field. Blackthorn sticks. Home and dry.

If you're sixteen, I must be three or four.
The combine harvester in McParland's haggard. The ricks sky high.

If I'm three or four, this must be the church in Eglish.
The elevation of the Host. Monstrance. Pyx. Sky high.

"God will lift off the great doors of heaven on threshing-day.
The wheat will fly clear of the great chaff-cutter. Home and dry."

This priest has a Derry accent, though. *You're* the four-year-old.
"Don't you need chaff," you're asking, "to make bricks? To build bricks sky
high?"

"That can't be right." Your father tut-tutting to his neighbor
at the Cookstown fair. "Half a crown for a dozen day-old chicks? Sky high."

The neighbor's my father, a servant boy
shouldering his creel of day-old chicks and butter home and dry.

My father at twelve, in the Odeon or the Ritz,
blazing his way into this new movie by Tom Mix, *Sky High*.

Your father overhearing an Orangeman on Craig and Carson.
"We've enough, after Larne, to blow these fucking Micks sky high."

"No Isaac Butters," another crows. "No Home Rule till Lough Neagh runs
dry."
The stress on "Butters," "Home" and "Dry."

Our fathers, or our grandfathers, cutting and castling turf
as Balfour and Churchill jack up their rhetoric sky high.

Our great-grandfathers after a night in Magherafelt or Draperstown.
Red eyes. Black tongues. Razor-nicks. Sky high.

Your great-great-grandfathers staring down from the bridge at Toome.
McCorley. McCracken. The French *charcutiers* home and dry.

Our great-great-grandfathers. Their grandfathers
at the walls of Rome. The hoisted head of Vercingetorix, sky high.

Throughout all this, the exaltation of miles of heather and gorse
by a laverock's little clucks and clicks. Sky high.

The crowd-hush. The hoisted head. The laverock's slow cadenza.
The football flap-flutters home and dry.

The hope, sky high, that poetry may transfigure.
The hope that poetry may transform, as well as transfix, sky high.

The hope against hope that, through this column of smoke
that hangs over Acheron or the Styx, sky high,

some solid Muldoon, some ferryman,
may bear us, in his narrow-keeled, square-sterned cutter, home and dry.

120

Summer Whites

I want old-fashioned metaphor; I dress in black.
My son was murdered. I bear witness in black.

The graveyard shocks with rampant green.
In a rusted chair sits grief, enormous in black.

Died July 16, 1983.
Navy's white headstone, christcross in black.

A cardinal flames—sudden visitation.
Holy spirit? Surcease from black?

Grackles keen in mad falsetto.
Treeful of banshees. Fracas in black.

It should be told, of course, in small details
and with restraint (artfulness in black).

He was a sailor in summer whites in a port city.
He was walking, streets dangerous in black.

The bullet entered right shoulder, ricocheted.
In the ground his dress blues decompose to black.

I am Isabel. He was Jerry John. The dead
are listening for their names, soundless in the black.

For the Love of Saints

The sky shifts pinks of light through louvered fingers
And in your hair the wind's like smoothing fingers.

No stained glass truth bleeds colors framed and patterned:
The tracing of this frame you drew with fingers.

Here rhythms evangelical belong
Where sounds of vowels stroke wounds like bruising fingers.

From beds of reds pull tulips by sheer handfuls
But in the vase arrange the blooms in fingers.

Give in, give in, to Gabriel's round lips!
And wetting each, blow every fluted finger!

I would whisper Jesus from his lonely bed;
New manuscripts I'd fold in Matthew's fingers.

No gospel love pours out of hands like oil
The way my words for you seep through these fingers.

How do you braid sixteen fingers in four hands?
The trick? She weaving yours, you weaving hers.

Sounds save us, too, as they seduce.
And ye shall find the babe in music's fingers.

So hold me, hands stained not with sin but juice:
Just as I am, hold berry-bloodied fingers.

Dreamers

My mother's standing pointing at the sky in a dream,
"Can you see it, there?" I hear her cry in a dream.

My head is in the clouds like yours. I know it now;
But you're the one to blame. I'm in a quandary, in a dream.

Give me the blank banked tall with vague immensities—
I too am racing, drifting, floating high in a dream.

I will never see things as you'd have me do,
Blood logic. Madness I defy in a dream.

Up there it's white, opaque. Like gauze the thought won't hold;
We fall through space discover we can fly in a dream.

Bears and whales and galleons. Heaven has a face.
The lover which we fail to place, identify in a dream.

The dead can speak. The sea divides. I am the bride.
And I don't need to find a reason why in a dream.

Insistence weighs but you must see we can't agree.
God will weep if we see eye-to-eye in a dream.

A mother and a daughter shouldn't be the same.
Panthers pace like jealousy that boundary in a dream.

Yes, I look like you. The mirror has your mouth.
It bit me once and now I am twice shy in a dream.

Simile is sucking at the source, the planetary curve
Of cheek and breast synonymous, you and I in a dream.

She is the judge. The jury too. I stand accused
Of crimes I half-remember and deny in a dream.

The stone will budge. You will be free when you, Peggy,
Grasp the solid truth you too will die in a dream.

Trust

Late at night, smoking hydroponic, Elvis is King
and you're right, I'm not there for the asking.

We're always open and you're always welcome
but I might, I must insist on a full-body frisking.

In an amber dusk I cast the shadow of your dreams.
In better light I stand tall as The Great Wuss King.

Dragging around the apartment, pale, mooning
the dim bright of the fridge is my only basking.

In the street, the movie line, the laundromat—
word fights with broken bones worth risking.

There were times I considered your banishment.
Late at night, drinking cold tonic, I was the last king.

Truth is a chalice we'd all like to drink from.
Well, not quite. James prefers a good masking.

Comet Ghazal

Amidst our troubles, a sudden blessing:
Look up. There's a comet in the evening sky.

An omen for a Pharoah, caught retracing
Its half-forgotten summit in the evening sky;

Two burning tails—one gas, one ice—arousing
Ancient tumult in the evening sky;

Debris of a lost planet decomposing;
Gypsy diplomat in the evening sky;

Debut of life on earth, its ice dispersing
Facts too intimate for the evening sky . . .

Traces of comet in us. This burning, this freezing?
Let's just blame it on the evening sky.

The music of the spheres in us, rehearsing
Across the gamut of the evening sky.

But—see?—the comet's already devising
A short-cut past the limit in the evening sky.

And when it comes again, we won't be witnessing
Who will even claim it in the evening sky?

What's left of us may well be improvising
Our own last-minute plummet in the evening sky.

The Dome

At times they will fly under. The dome
contains jungles. Invent a sky under the dome.

Creatures awake, asleep, at play, aglow:
They float—unbottled genii—under the dome.

Southern Belle, a splash of black, dusted with gold,
dissembles, "assembling," acts shy under the dome.

Cattleheart, Giant Swallowtail, Clipper:
Sail, navigate sky high under the dome.

Like confetti—a wedding—bits of Rice
Paper: sheer mimicry under the dome.

Magnificent Owl, in air, a pansy,
it feeds, wings up, eye to eye, under the dome.

Name them: Monarch, then Queen, last Viceroy.
What will scientists deify under the dome?

Basking against a leaf: a Banded Orange,
displayed like a bowtie under the dome.

A living museum. Exist to be observed:
Never migrate, but live, then die, under the dome.

Lips, lashes, eyes. From the outside in
Do beings magnify under the dome?

Lepidoptera. From the Greek: Scale-wing.
Chysalis. Stay, butterfly, under the dome.

Sam's Ghazal

You're out. The house is dead. With me:
you're safe. Why not stay home, instead, with me?

That Ur prince whisked you off past four.
At my leash-end, you're not misled by me.

He's like a tide. He comes. He goes.
I'm always here. Life's anchored with me.

My needs are few: a bowl, a lead, some love.
You won't get in the red with me.

You never have to cook, just pop a Mighty Dog:
a snap to have breakfasted with me.

He paws, he yaps, he barely listens.
I'm all ears. Much is left unsaid with me.

Maybe I have my quirks (stairs scare, streets clank),
but you've always kept your head with me.

He is six foot one. I am one foot high.
Don't ever let him tread on me.

Though small, I claim my space and like you snug.
(It's tough sharing a bed with me.)

My name is Samson. Yours is Paschen.
So keep your name and stay unwed with me.

—Sam

The Flight

A broken star, a lost eye, sorrow on loan as it leaves you.
Who doesn't know such absences? The groan as it leaves you?

More fallen each day, peace is more exalted in its failures—the boy
gunned down on the road, then mourned alone as it leaves you.

Peace offers what then? Hope like a flag, or the close presence
of a room—dark with a mahogany drone as it leaves you?

We court the hills and court the sea. We fly to the moon, wrest
one word from another, try to make it a home as it leaves you.

I too watched a ship go down in the dazzle of the sea—*radiant matter*
covering my breasts—sidereal enclosure—*love* intoned as it leaves you.

Snow. Desert. Sea. The mystics came, wept to see. Suffering's
their art, chord to heaven—not yours to claim or condone as it leaves you.

Cathedrals of pine, rock, of city dwellings—you know these places.
Good and evil coupled in a world only known as it leaves you?

The dove confused your heart. The ship went down. Snow. Desert.
Sorrow of heaven. What else do you expect to own as it leaves you?

The light embraces the leaf, the dark belongs to night. Even in sleep,
Peg, in snow, in sea—*the radiant matter*—the dove's alone as it leaves
you.

In Open Meadow

Miss Crabtree led us past the fishery to here—in open meadow:
"children, blue . . . blue heron flying without fear in open meadow!"

Your sleeping brow + the kiss of dewy lips = a hieroglyphic.
How many soft prints of young deer in open meadow?

Farther you are undone; we gather geraniums and wait.
The Japanese King? A vigil for frailty: Sleep, Lear in open meadow.

Oh, help yourself to seconds of: was/is/am/have/been/shall/will be;
And others? Nothing need be austere in open meadow.

Poor Isadora unnerved. The dance "striptease was ill received."
A tarot pack critic could see "something queer in open meadow."

Summer rain changed to hail, wailing flowers bent—
Black-eyed Susan gales: ". . . at last the Queen disappears in open
                                                                    meadow . . ."

And what advice, Teresa, did the poet offer? "Hurry up, it's time:
Return to a place lit by a glass from Kashmir in open meadow."

Ghazal

Pausing for ecstasy at the shore tomorrow?
Love, you will find quicksand for a floor tomorrow.

Pee Wee's ambiguity led to hot debate.
Who would be Hollywood's new kore tomorrow?

That Sicilian summer you stole my figs, "Forgive,"
you said, "I'll find my composure tomorrow."

Poor Yorrick, served-up as a "gentle reminder":
we know the worm eats at the core tomorrow.

Someone plucked the Egret tail feather from her hat;
the chivalrous heart would settle the score tomorrow.

Clouds move brilliantly across the moon
and yes, there will be someone to adore tomorrow.

Oh, to corrupt the man with the garlic wagon,
his lineage, all his fruits and more tomorrow!

August peonies thrive until the hour of rain: petal
strewn lawn. And for us? What may be in store tomorrow?

Complaint: Beloved groom, I am Teresa, my namesake of Avila,
but not a castle found today (and some say) nor tomorrow.

Wight

In the dark we disappear, pure being.
Our mirror images, impure being.

Being and becoming (Heidegger), being and
nothingness (Sartre)—which is purer being?

Being alone is no way to be: thus
loneliness is the test of pure being.

Nights in love I fell too far or not quite
far enough—one pure, one impure being.

Clouds, snow, mist, the dragon's breath on water,
smoke from fire—a metaphor's pure being.

Stillness and more stillness and the light locked
deep inside—both pure and impure being.

Is it the verb of being, I the noun—
or pronoun for the purists of being.

I was, I am, I looked within and saw
nothing very clearly: purest being.

Polio

Those humid hours that lingered on for days.
The body stretched in breathlessness for days.

In Ohio *dies caniculares*
meant something: virus, Sirius, Dog Star days.

Whatever it was was like catching cold.
Bad headaches, swelling, fevers, chills for days.

(The boy in braces for the March of Dimes
lurched toward the lights of the camera dazed.)

When the night sky cleared of vapor: there
in Canis Major the stars that fixed our days.

We knew if we died we could join these stars.
For the girl in the iron lung *dies* were days.

We knew if we survived past Labor Day, then school:
another year of colds and growing pains for days.

Oranges

When winter ratchets down its crunch-bone cold, oranges
provide our talisman, our bough of gold, oranges.

They are not rare, as in our parents' shared anecdotes,
exotic gifts a stocking toe might hold, oranges.

Thin-skinned and rich in oils, blue-ribbon specimens,
perfume the fingertips when palmed and rolled, oranges.

Girdled by four equators, pared meticulously,
eight petals curl, disclose the pulp, unfold oranges.

Segments divide, cathedral window-stained translucency
bursts on the tongue; heart hungers are consoled, oranges.

Papaya, mango, carabóla, persimmon
forsworn, we load the cargo bay with cold oranges.

Let the Olympians brag their nectar, their ambrosia.
Our feast is not less rightfully extolled, oranges.

Barefoot, we trod where warm waves wreathed our ankle bones
and bobbed with windfalls. From those waves we trolled oranges.

Make no mistake. Such food as feeds and cheers is luxury,
however cheap or dear or freely doled: oranges.

Indentured pickers work for pittance. Little changes
since wenches hawked, by stage-lamp, bawdy-bold, oranges.

What renders living graciously exploitative;
the justice-lover, moralistic scold? Oranges?

Thus cries the roving minstrel, "Sweet or sour or contraband—
come buy my wares, if you can be cajoled: oranges."

Regret

Who has not sometimes longed to heave regret
over the rail, deep-six it, leave regret?

Why rue the days? Or would life lose its edge
if our charmed souls could not conceive regret?

What pains us? Losses, errors, harmful deeds?
Could workshops teach us not to grieve? Regret?

We half admire villains, monsters, those
who, in defeat, cannot achieve regret.

Which is more base, to feign a glorious past
or wallow in Walpurgis Eve regret?

Within the opulence of memory,
what waywardness to mow and sheave regret!

Good people, living useful, noble lives,
infect declining years and weave regret.

But if repentance and self-pity blend,
it may be time to strike and cleave regret.

Oblivion or contrition? Given the choice,
might we still hanker to retrieve regret?

On the continuum of conscience, shun
both utter woe and petty peeve regret.

I cherish equipoise, but if you ask
my name, I wear it on my sleeve, Regret.

Ghazals

What treasures can one find in Arabic?
God's footprints left behind in Arabic.

Amherst: winter scribbles on the pane
the autographs of angels, signed in Arabic.

The heart's anomalies, x-rays confirm,
can only be defined in Arabic.

The riddle posed at sleep's unyielding gate
will readily unwind in Arabic.

Translations tangle warp and ravel weft:
The truth is best confined to Arabic.

    * * *

The faces fade from your dreams in Arabic,
each absence a reproach in Arabic.

The foreign ear is sleeping: war's alarms
are poetry when raised in Arabic

One called *Beloved* bears a secret scar
where God has signed his name in Arabic.

Though *glare* and *rime* play on the exile's tongue;
There are no words for them in Arabic.

The wanderer from the countryside has come
who can translate the rain from Arabic.

(Un)Mask

What's wanted here are sensibilities:
no logic, but clear sensibilities

Could you just this once speak plain English, please?
Forget your vaunted sensibilities.

Your lover plays to your proclivities:
less clothing than is sensible, a tease.

Sleeping, young turk, awaking, *éminence grise*:
the shift a jolt to sensibilities.

Still sleek and hungry: though satiety's
what most mark, some can sense abilities.

In your convictions, cold sobriety's
no substitute for sensibilities.

Burnished bronze gives way to verdigris's
cool green to soothe your sensibilities.

It was an ill-tuned reed concocted these
ghazals to try your sensibilities.

Air Raid

Lighter than water, heavier than air,
you break the surface, filling your lungs with air.

Three of a kind will always beat two pair:
you hole card's disappeared into thin air.

Perhaps you just imagined it was there,
dreaming a dragonfly leaning on the air.

Once surrounded by an ether sphere,
we now look for protection to the air.

Feathers become dark smoke and disappear:
one sign of angels fallen from the air.

Adam and Eve were said to be such a pair—
Unconscious of their beauty, clothed in air.

Rumors abound, confirmations are rare,
proof is evanescent as the air.

Flesh and blood could not hope to compare
with dreams as insubstantial as the air.

Waterfall

From pole to pole, nothing in place but water,
yet God was moving on the face of water.

Pulling abreast, you're sure that you have caught her.
You lunge, and she slips through your hands like water.

Careful to cross her *t*s, sure to dot her
is—in vain; she has no ink but water.

The ocean is more palimpsest than blotter:
every mistake is captured in the water.

Around the frame you mark the sign of slaughter.
This blood will never wash away in water.

On the Wing

You fly to my table with unbuttoned sleeves.
You look like an angel with unbuttoned sleeves.

Where have you been? Did you run from a fire?
Here, share my meal with unbuttoned sleeves.

Like a page dipped in ink, your cuff's in my coffee.
You have something to tell with unbuttoned sleeves.

Don't say it yet. That's not what you mean.
I know you too well with unbuttoned sleeves.

How many years since I first loved your face?
You could have set sail with unbuttoned sleeves.

Clothes make the man. Our bed's still unmade.
Please pay the bill with unbuttoned sleeves.

Unbutton me back to our first nakedness.
I have no name at all with unbuttoned sleeves.

Prayer

Yom Kippur: wearing a bride's dress bought in Jerusalem,
I peer through swamp reeds, my thought in Jerusalem.

Velvet on grass. Odd, but I learned young to keep this day
just as I can, if not as I ought, in Jerusalem.

Like sleep or love, prayer may surprise the woman
who laughs by a stream, or the child distraught in Jerusalem.

My dress is Arabic: spangles, blue-green-yellow beads
the shades of mosaics hand-wrought in Jerusalem

Jews, Muslims, prize, like the blue-yellow Dome of the Rock;
like strung beads-and-cloves said to ward off the drought in Jerusalem.

Both savor things that grow wild—coreopsis in April,
the rose that buds late, like an afterthought, in Jerusalem.

While car-bombs flared, an Arab poet translated
Hebrew verse whose flame caught in Jerusalem.

And you, Shahid, said Judah Halevi's sea as I,
on Ghalib's, course like an Argonaut in Jerusalem.

Stone lions pace the Sultan's gate while almonds bloom
into images, Hebrew and Arabic, wrought in Jerusalem.

No words, no metaphors, for guns that sear flesh
on streets where the people have fought in Jerusalem.

As this spider weaves a web in silence,
may Hebrew and Arabic be woven taut in Jerusalem.

Here at the bay, I see my face in the shallows
and plumb for the true self our Abraham sought in Jerusalem.

Open the gates to rainbow-colored words
of outlanders, their sounds untaught in Jerusalem.

My name is Grace, Chana in Hebrew—and in Arabic.
May its meaning, "God's love," at last be taught in Jerusalem.

Soup

Poets are poor, air in the cupboard, we try soup;
Hatted man chomps buzzard drumstick, and asks Why soup?

Broken pencils, brazen bulbs, cracked dishes, clutter—
We live on dirty pawprints, paper, nails, and soup.

Croaking love, the bird swept through and pecked at my heart.
It left nothing except an acorn in my soup.

Around the creaking hut the wind lashes the bush—
I wander on Desolation Ranch, and make soup.

Of course my life could be more velvet, more padding,
But boot toes in leaves, Sagaree stands and stirs soup.

Ghazal of Perfume

Does anyone understand the perfume?
It drives a man & a woman to a room.

Afraid that you will like it too much?
Then take no woman, no man to a room.

Does anyone hear the rustle of skin?
A man & a woman are in a room.

She's dressed in black; she glows with care.
A woman has a man in her room.

When do we experience the woe of sex?
A woman has no man in her room.

When do we experience the woe of sex?
A man has no woman in his room.

The moon is angry; there is no perfume?
A man & a woman have left the room.

Covenant

Even as I grasp this pen, its intimate world,
I unloosen myself from the deliberate world.

The tanager can't see his beauty, just danger.
Each creature's *atman* shines as an animate world.

Sap traps a fruitfly for a thousand and one years.
Its amber death still mirrors a duplicate world.

I've lived long enough to invite fire to my bed.
Now ashes fill my mouth with a surrogate world.

If I could fly, I'd soar inward, a spear speeding
Its lightning to pierce each heart's immaculate world.

Screech of jay, sting of wasp, a sharply whittled pain
In the breast reminds flesh of its intricate world.

Watery dreams move within my darkening veins—
Gold streams radiate beneath the desolate world.

Time is both savage and kind, a blind prophet who
Reveals visions, who invokes a disparate world.

Savor the fragrance of lily and lavender.
They unfurl the wisdom of God's delicate world.

Undone my sureties of self and soul and tongue:
I release myself to the inebriate world.

Why, Maurya, insist upon singing in the dark?
Silence and light ignite the elaborate world.

Ghazal

With the rage and longing you'd see in a hurt child,
I challenge heaven with my plea of a hurt child.

Is the rest of his life an afterthought, a footnote:
the psychopathology of the hurt child?

There is always that connection, an iron bond,
"or leather, let it be," says the hurt child.

Others, more gently reared, may misconstrue,
but the world is harsh. "Trust me," says the hurt child.

But afterward, the remorse, on both sides, and the love
the others can scarcely imagine, and they envy the hurt child.

Think of David's love for his son, and Absalom's for him.
In that reciprocity is the hurt, child.

Incarnation

She wasn't looking when she said Jesus
Filled her with the quick and dead. Jesus!

The cop who laughed *Revival!* was like the John
Who preceded and heralded Jesus.

When she met the gentle man who would be
Her husband, she thought: Take to bed Jesus!

(The incarnation, she explained, meant sex
Could not have truly limited Jesus.)

But, oh, he was sorry! It didn't take
Her long to see she hadn't wed Jesus.

Only her faith in herself was shaken.
Magdalene hadn't merited Jesus.

A child came. He drank even more. Then left.
I got to, she scrawled, go to spread Jesus.

She'd hear the stories of healings and signs.
She felt sick he'd discredited Jesus.

He'd show up drunk with those big eyes and she'd
Give in. But he never could shed Jesus.

Of course, he finally overdid spirits,
Was found palms up like the outspread Jesus.

So many children. Some died in the war,
Some in bars, fast cars. Some born dead. Jesus.

She was angry sometimes and sometimes scared
To think the schools prohibited Jesus.

I told her I believed—but I didn't
Fool her. Ron, she said, don't you dread Jesus?

Finally

My friend was finally going to write those poems.
The mortician asked me why he chose poems.

No money in it, he said. Why not novels?
The truly living, I said, can't close poems.

He'd done a few in his youth, quite fine pieces.
You can ask someone who really knows poems.

I had him burned. Then poured him on the rapids.
(Earth wheels fat narratives, but it slows poems.)

He himself the round world, Falstaffian, was
Suddenly Gloucester, blind, trying to nose poems.

Why toe the line? The shit of daily life can
Fertilize, at best, only prose poems.

He said to me once, Ron, you understand I
Should give up all this for sweet woes, poems.

Royal

We are one of those long-married couples who do not speak.
Especially after our argument on the train to Brighton, we do not speak.

For the life of me, I can't read a timetable, while my husband can.
Around us, elderly couples lift pasty faces to sun, and do not speak.

I order Earl Grey with milk and sugar, and creme-filled biscuits.
Reclining on green and white-striped lawn chairs, we still do not speak.

We visit the Royal Palace where King George IV summered.
I wonder if, like exhausted marrieds, kings and queens do not speak.

Among regal objets d'art, were they ever pierced through the heart?
Or suffer emotional pains about which the English do not speak?

I, Carole, an American, understand little of royal restraint.
I am myself a ruined soul, with wild fantasies I do not speak.

Old-Stuff Ghazal

His turnout—disarray! So long
a phase. He's been blasé so long.

His stuff's old. Nothing's up-to-date.
He's had that Chevrolet so long.

No fashion sense at all, alas.
His wardrobe's been passé so long.

His grooming is not up-to-snuff—
His hair hangs lank and gray—so long.

Maybe he'll ask her for a date—
Send a communiqué so long—

Detailing his plans to play croquet,
view etchings on display so long.

Of course, she wants to be polite.
Says she can only stay so long.

She's through with couplets—any kind—
It's late, she's tired, she'll say, So long!

With Insomnia Goes Imagination

I consider my life while my puppy twitches in deepest sleep.
A few years back, I'd have anxiously coveted her sleep.

Now I'm well-rested but deaf to those 2 a.m. songs.
I try to write poems, but my muse has fallen dead or asleep.

The doctor of Chinese medicine inquires after my dreams.
I can't think of *any*, as if the back of my head were asleep.

My dog shakes a leg, chomps at air, squeaks at nothing in sight.
She's chasing a bear and racing a sled in her sleep.

On paper I note that I've answered my life's basic needs.
That means work, home, love, dog, bread, water, sleep.

There's nothing I miss but the circling birds in my brain.
Now, when I'm tired, I curl up, like a dog, in my bed and sleep.

The silence is huge. The only voice is the one that declares:
Adrienne, this was your wish. All you ever wanted was sleep.

No Palms

No palms dolled up the tedium, no breathing wind.
No problem was the buzzword then, their way to go.

In truth, my case was black as sin, a thing to hide,
In that they feigned to find me sane, so not to know.

Someone brought in a medium. Anathema!
Some clown sewed up my eyes, he said it wouldn't show.

Confusing hand with craze, they howled, "Let's cut them off."
Confusing, too, their spies, my lies without an echo.

Time and again they stitched my mind with warp and woof.
Time pounded in my grubby heart, doing a slow,

Slow dim-out in that lupanar, slow take, slow fade,
slow yawning like a door. "Hello," I said "HELLO."

There, flung across the room between inside and out,
There must have shown itself to me . . . an afterglow.

With such a blaze to celebrate where centuries meet
With time itself, how could I hesitate? Although

Still trapped in the millenium I knew I had
still time to blow some kisses. Look up, there they go!

Famous Pairs

Adam and Eve walked around paradise, innocent, in the dark.
One bite: the Fall, then misery, and Satan creeps in the dark.

Mark Antony's gone. Cleopatra puts the asp to her breast.
Iris, Charmian expire. Cleo dies too. The snake's replete in the dark.

All Salem's come out to gawk at Hester's fashion statement.
Her sins exposed while Dimmesdale clasps his secret in the dark.

Mimi needs a little oil for her lamp and Rudolph's happy to supply.
But love can't cure that cough. Forever she sleeps in the dark.

Charles Baudelaire loves Jeanne Duval. Hates her too:
she's panther, incubus, vampire who shrieks in the dark.

Marcel waits impatiently in bed for his Mother's kiss.
A footstep! Here she is! Still, his heart's incomplete in the dark.

When Anaïs met Henry, it was like looking in a mirror—
Lust or vanity? Is it self-love or sympathy that speaks in the dark?

Holofernes the Assyrian beds Judith and gets a big surprise.
She'd said, "Shall I lie down with you, my sweet? In the dark?"

Broken Ghazal

Weeks afterward, the pieces were still falling out;
They looked like bits of pink sponge and kept coming out.

I will establish control of my surroundings—I have a sponge.
This place just needs a bit of wiping and good sweeping out.

When the tent flaps down, you can see what's going on;
When the box is opened, the jester comes popping out.

No, I don't use the sidewalk, and I don't walk on the lawn;
I also don't use doors or stairs—what's the use of going out.

Sometimes I visit the garden to see the manticore,
Sometimes to see the peony buds—so slow, but bursting out.

You ask, do I have a lover? I close the tongs.
Only this blue ring burns for me; bring tea, I'm running out.

You ask what she was to me, and I say we shared a room.
It's all sepia now, but then it was a flood-plain spilling out.

Pouring the Wine

A light slashes through pines into the world.
Cities lift their spines into the world.

All things are echoes. A line becomes the Nile.
The Nile bears all that shines into the world.

Bear down, dig in. Delve into love's defile.
Pull the ore from mines into the world.

You are my voice, my eyes, my feet, my hands.
Inject my anodynes into the world.

All things are signs. Sing, my tall friend.
Pour the mystic wines into the world.

The Window

I sit by this clear square of the world
And watch the changing glare of the world.

Sunrise slowly threads itself through
Trees whose black arms tear at the world.

Headlines crackle on the floor beneath
The sprawling cat, unaware of the world.

A north wind rolls from tree to tree
Chasing its tail of air through the world.

Above the field, a far-off plane
Hums its one note of despair to the world.

Now pink, now orange, the sun at length
Suspends its long affair with the world.

The square goes black. A pale moon-face
Bends close, returns the stare from the world.

I know her look, her eyes, her palms
Press mine in sudden prayer for the world.

Ghazal of the Winter Storm

The fire's out. I wish you could come home.
Moonlight calms the gate where you stumbled. Come home.

When rations are lifted we'll cook all day
and never mind the heat that out of hell comes home.

The plates, piled high with meat, the tumblers
we pull from shelves, the table, all call come home.

Pie will fill your mouth, toothsome apple I plucked
from the tree which each fall comes home.

Even the dog misses you, that you kicked
until he bled, and sends his humble come home.

I never meant to send you into snow that day.
One step away's the fire's anvil: come home.

Himalaya

Branches: wings: we sheltered in thick fir trees.
The cliff-face, as we'd asked, had furnished trees.

When your mother died, I dreamed the wild mountain
of the grave, its myrrh and milk, fur and fleece.

I know what my soul saw: the sky like silk
pulled through a ring, a flock of wind-slurred trees.

Those feathery evergreens were blue—didn't you
wear blue for luck at all her surgeries?

Calm came into the dream, unburdened, as snow.
It sugared the rocks, the rock-encircled trees.

Lost souls can make themselves be known. Wind stirs
the snow, and shakes our murderous certainties.

Regret came into the dream thankless as snow.
It floured God's black beard, it furred the trees.

Years past, a soul slipped by the stone I was.
On the windowpane, frost's rucked embroideries.

Root and branch: the year of fasting ends.
Outside: veiled sun, snow's layered silks, blurred trees.

Whose ghost is it, Shahid, feeds my grief dream?
Whose loss, whose task, whose darkened nursery?

Ghazal

Late November. On the sill: three leaves.
Puddled beneath the tree. Leaves.

Are roots, long life, a form of bondage?
Small wonder the winds free leaves.

Beware your blindness, your science.
Look (cold days) to dreams, tea leaves.

A tethered hawk won't ignore spring wind.
Eyes hooded, he'll still see leaves.

No remedy to cure your absence.
Light, talk, dark. Nothing relieves.

Did we forget the play beneath work,
covered as a child in the leaves?

Daylight, like a poem, fades to end.
The poet is the sun. He leaves.

Side Street

> "Controlled Movement": the regulation of passage, at specified intervals, from
> one building to another in Massachusetts prisons.

Controlled Movement is the new step we dance down America Lane:
a beat, a policy, a correctional mandate laid on America Lane.

Who controls the movement? Chairman, forewoman, clock,
market research, poetic law, referendum: all fashion America Lane.

Someone has planted nubble marigolds along the chartered plots:
slattern zinnias, petunias, pansies line America Lane.

"Keep moving," snaps the guard, "or it's solitary," swivelling his eye
at the inmates, denimed and sullen, who trudge on America Lane.

Neon bleeds down the boulevards, Dijonnaise drools over chard,
the chairman lights up, glasses twinkle, logos shine: America Lane.

"Nothing is more fertile in marvels," says Tocqueville, "than the art
of being free; but nothing is harder to learn." Our lesson: America Lane.

"A car chase," demands the director, "Something expansive, expensive, hot.
Smash ten Pontiacs, blow up a jeep." "Who pays?" Groan: "America Lane."

I went looking in gunshops and delis, car lots, high rises, bars,
in libraries, church cloakrooms, the nature reserve: Salon America Lane.

Directions: take any side street, turn left at the fence with the swaying rose.
I swear, that's really the name of the road to the prison: America Lane.

In Bogs

There is evidence for ancient lakes lying innate in bogs.
There is remedy for arthritic aches lying sedate in bogs.

An high-tech peat heats Irish homes and improves young modern lives—
the children run dry through dust bowls where their parents walked wet
in bogs.

Israel's Children, with harnessed might, marched onward to Sinai,
while Pharoah's forces, through an oversight, found themselves trapped
in bogs.

The will-o-the-wisp we watched last night was nomadic and man-made
—a psychic called in by police had said "Search for her in bogs."

He is a shaman, of good intent; his forebears—Wolf and Crow.
And I am Watkins, of Welsh descent, so my forebears rest in bogs.

At Night

Not all rivers during winter are frozen deep at night
—the juice of lovers, rich or poor, begins to seep at night.

At ten o'clock, in most large towns, the graveyard shift begins
—the junkie whores, divine in service, earn their keep at night.

Some senate creep passes a bill to "rid the streets of filth";
his teenage daughter, feeling his breath, starts to weep at night.

Miss Canada, the wholesome Plaything, dreams of movie deals,
while the stripper, with her thoughts of Dad, cannot sleep at night.

My good friend Wren, in bed by ten, still mourns her father's death;
while myself, Robert, contemplate the wounds we reap at night.

Ghazal

Newly happy in my body, blind to the lie at the core,
I play with forbidden self, tantalized to the core.

She lurches from black tights & "creative movement"
to pink and a bun: how will she find her "I" in *the corps*?

Kelly blades growing from cindars: some call dubious
proof there's new life in what dies at the core.

Are waves deaf? Asks Michaux. Sometimes it's
other's music we covet—to get a rise at the core.

Teen-angry, innocent of what "it" was, I yelled *Eat it raw*!
Among the underpants they found a good-sized apple core.

For days she's acted years older; when she starts sobbing
I'm lost to *my* effort not to capsize at the core.

Songs we mumble, melodies we hum, dreams burrowing
upwards—hints for who listens: noise from the core.

I bloom to the click & thrill of a stranger, then flood
with blue-ish relief: he's not my size at the core.

Gutter is a word hurled: who lives there is tattered.
But aren't we "owners" uncivilized at the core?

Fire doesn't know how to be small for five minutes. No
apology blooms from his mouth, I ignite at the core.

In search of seals, beach glass, shooting stars, we go
from zoom-mode to wide-angle: we have eyes at the core.

In the wake of my leaving, no sleep—but at dawn
I find I still smell of last night at the core.

Dream: I eat the shelled egg a white hen offers held
in her claw-foot. We are all disguised to the core.

Rilke's Angels

Barber of split hairs re-fusing at death,
I have learned refusal from Rilke's angels.

Skimmer of all he reads into the universe,
I have been apprenticed in perusal by Rilke's angels.

Student of crotch-rot in sugar loaded diabetics,
I have dismembered that puzzle with Rilke's angels.

They limn some perfect form divinely intended
For only the razzle-dazzle of Rilkean angels.

Bring me a belated sedative in mimicry
From those experts in despisal-arousal, Rilke's angels.

I know what they're stuck on, yet over umpteen years
Have groped in vain for the easels of Rilke's angels.

Their loveliness, all molten embrocation,
Belies the cold-cut carousals of Rilke's angels.

In the end I have come to know by heart
Only the consternated, aloof frazzles of Rilke's angels.

Amid buzzing liquids forced into ultimate being
I am the western pall-bearer who guzzles Rilke's angels.

Autumn

I'm always in a good mood on the first days of autumn,
unable to do much but brood on the first days of autumn.

Shivering trees lined the streets where I wandered,
married to solitude on the first days of autumn.

All summer I swore I'd lost all hope—but there is no sight
sadder than a bitter prude on the first days of autumn.

The self I pieced together from a million *don'ts* and *cannots*
comes so wonderfully unglued on the first days of autumn.

All is fullness, ripeness, lushness. How badly I long to spill
the juices in which I've stewed on the first days of autumn!

I will go down the path the fallen leaves make, a carpet
inviting and crimson-hued, on the first days of autumn.

How fast my thoughts race on these gusty, raw evenings;
how fine to be wooed on the first days of autumn.

But for every new door the wind blows open,
an old fear is renewed on the first days of autumn.

Will the couples who fight through the long, hard winter
be the same ones who billed and cooed on the first days of autumn?

Chilly hints of coming darkness—is it wrong
not to feel somewhat subdued on the first days of autumn?

Mountains of snow will bury me soon enough;
let no more cold blasts intrude on the first days of autumn.

Even in this wild city, where frowns make such good armor,
we're all too thrilled to be rude on the first days of autumn.

Lost Letter

I'm your letter lost here in Maine
My ink a blackened smear in Maine

No sleep in the moon's silver eye
Giggling loons mock my fear in Maine

Composed then crumpled by cold hands
Red tree drops a red tear in Maine

Sweet cutting lines dissected me
Does holy flesh disappear in Maine

Did you smile headlining my name
John, dear John, severed ear in Maine

Nocturne

My heart's shy as a deer in Maine
Not wise to love a queer in Maine

Though Moby's white Flank long gone
Each cop carries a spear in Maine

In Portland they toss us from bridges
Sailor humping must disappear in Maine

No romping neath the moon's yellow eye
Pleasure cruises austere in Maine

Still I hunt you in dark woods and streets
Fuck killers stalking fear in Maine

End Without World

Here where the land sinks to make the sea the world
I devise to make your hand above my knee, the world.

A blackened window, God only god, full and empty,
time outside time, somehow unraveled to be the world.

Often I think our lives are mistakes memorized, or
a play we watch and pretend we see the world.

Money slams doors. In the alley, next to the dumpster,
a bum without a nose. How can we rekey the world?

Darkness, rough blankets, hard, bare floor. In this
room, alone in alone, you still furnish me the world.

Much we should have done and shouldn't. We shall be God
for forgiveness when God says "Forgive me the world."

Bruce, see the spider weave across the opening,
try again, now, in this body, slowly, free the world.

Ghazal of Faithfulness

I kiss your mouth in the face of someone else.
Is this you on my hand, this taste of someone else?

Pay me. Money is not paper, metal, symbol, but
sweat, bone, the shared space of someone else.

Much music seeps through the wall: pink, yellow
flowers overflow the vase of someone else.

Angels are sexless or completely sexed. They fuck
till their being takes the place of someone else?

Do you want wine? Shall I bring drugs? How can I
change my words to the verse of someone else?

In the morning, sun permeates the shade like liquor,
smoke, the stained smell on lace of someone else.

The beloved is not beloved. Must I say this? Do you
learn nothing sweating in the embrace of someone else?

He taught us we were unique, as a handprint—how
touching. Now he's replaced by someone else.

She'll never use your name, Bruce, write it here.
Rub it down below the waist of someone else.

Ghazal

Risk it? What, after all, have you got to lose?
With a time-honored form, you ought to lose.

The gambling fever rises: the wheel, a dervish, spins.
Tempt fate. You feel too hot to lose.

Never mind if you sense yourself losing your grip—
When wrestling angels, you've fought to lose.

Is it the Belovéd's dear form, glimpsed in the crowd?
What the heart most desires, you're taught to lose.

Apollo's statue has no flaw. Its pose is final.
Such cold and marble laws you sought to lose.

You mourn for, adore, those your ancestors killed.
To relinquish victory is not to lose.

Sun and wind, space: a mirror turns on a string.
The empty mind's best: all thought to lose.

When the soul slips its mooring, it leaves language behind.
So, forgetting the game, you forgot to lose.

In all transparent modesty, you drop your name.
For Eleanor is not a lot to lose.

Ghazal

For DA

Today, my friend, when all the scarified world implies a web,
This *ghazal*'s for you, who told me that word signifies a "web."

The Tigris's meandering lingo's far from my rap city's.
And yet beneath each culture's rhapsodies there lies a web.

You know, because he was a weaver too, that Webster knew,
Because all languages are foreign, that they comprise a web.

Cow pat, *Kuhhandel*, cow's parsley, *la voie lactée*, it's all a mesh.
Look closely at the wings: each dung-drawn, web-doomed fly's a web.

From their own pincerlike, pararachnid vantages,
Dictators like Saddam presume to supervise a web.

My friend, whose name, suppressed perforce, means something like
                                                    physician,
Vesalius has shown how selfness must disguise a web.

When Gertrude Stein saw suddenly "the difference is spreading,"
Her dictum covered all the acts from which arise a web.

Now here I am, giddy in Yiddish, dizzy with *ghazal*-dazzle,
Arch fornicator, delighted that he multiplies a web.

Eating the Season

I said I had an urge to greet the spring
And you misheard me, asking "Eat the spring?"

I laughed. "What restaurant features that?"
Special Today! Our Rarest Treat: The Spring.

"You'd probably consume it if you could,"
You charged, "if it would help you to defeat the spring."

"Ah, no. Although I always find I wish
Inside myself, I could repeat the spring.

Who wouldn't emulate its raw displays,
Making the red one green, complete: *the spring?*"

And so we talked, as it went on and on,
Majestic, heady and discreet . . . The Spring.

How Many Bouquets?

The lover holds the letter in the palm of his hand.
Unread it flatters as it wilts in his hand.

There are oceans to cross but the harbor is sealed.
Why not, she said, pick up shells from my hand?

Bejeweled the queen makes a tragic false start.
Her consort, resigned, plays the card in his hand.

It is bewitched, the child cries out to her nanny,
Who laughs as the parrot eats from her hand.

There are eels, a dead whale, a voice in the sand.
Will Poe kiss the unringed, quivering, ghostlike hand?

She is cold in her bed and the butler with tea
Wavers once, wavers twice, spills the tea on her hand.

It is the story of the rose. How many bouquets?
The tide slaps the oozing sand. Unmanned, he slaps her hand.

Intervals

High flood returns, gradually drains off to the dead slack of time.
Another desert blows over another lost track of time.

When she wants to stay lost, her own mother's vibrant nerves sputter,
catch nothing but the faint twinge, hint, flicker, whiff and smack of time.

When she wants to get found, long backslashes of ocean rear up,
overturn, slosh her slight ruins up along the wrack of time.

Nighttime: groupers and angels sleep in the reef; crustaceans walk.
Or she and lively lizards dart across the forked crack of time.

Poor sunken ships! deaf gone dumb to the humpbacks' consultation.
Canyon rim—listen: wolfish Alpha howls in the pack of time.

Face to what face, who inhabits these colossal kelp forests?
Or a campfire sparks the battered moon, blue of and black of time.

To this day, as glaciers drop new calves into the knocking sea,
cubs try the incisive sabertoothed snicker and snack of time.

No uproar hurries her, salt gale or sandstorm mounted upwind—
maybe her burro licked up the last lingering lack of time.

Porpoise to wildebeest, no mother taught her those two tokens,
tick and tock, or tucked her in against any attack of time.

Fancy eye, the crow picks over her dust patch for curios,
pecks at glints nimbly switching glints in the nick and knack of time.

Consider Martha, who sometimes parches to death, or else drowns:
bounced out the front, she ducks around, back in at the back of time.

After Words

Ideas of Order in an Afterword

A volume of poetry denies the necessity of an aftermath. It declares itself as its own order, or an irrevocable logic that will happily forget a framework of either introductions or conclusions. The poems belong to a manifestation that—luckily—declares an indifference both to a "Once upon a time" beginning and to the false comfort of a "The End." Why, then, are these bodies of poems, these inhabitants, housed between introductory prose and concluding prose? Why, in other words, Agha Shahid Ali? And why me? Neither of us is quite comfortable with the literary situation of being merely footnotes, nor of the task of being explicators either before or after the fact of language. Why do we choose to put ourselves in this position that is so awkwardly gendered?

The answer is simple: It bespeaks the ravishment of form. That the formality involved is also a cultural condition—certainly connected with an engaged sense of pained translation—reiterates our historical connection with the formal beauty attached to the ghazal. My invocation of aesthetics is hardly incidental, since the delicacy of form is precisely the miracle of the ghazal, which has allowed in its scope decadence, mysticism, history, and politics—within the elegant construction of a single line.

A ghazal: On one level, it is just a formal house. It is a home that requires internal rhyme, always asking questions of the inevitable refrain. Since I am allergic to the misuses put to the term "couplet," I refuse to refer to the ghazal as a series of couplets, accommodating rhyme and refrain, and usually—but not always—concluding with two haunting lines that enclose, as a child, the poet's name. It would be a gross misunderstanding of the home to correlate this name with a vague gesture towards a nom de plume. Instead, the formal reversion in the final lines of the poem from the first to the third person is an invocation of tragedy that certainly exceeds what may be called a signature. An end is not in sight. The very structure of the poem disallows closure. Names are named much as children are named, who must remain parentless.

This collection therefore embodies an orphanage in which experiments must happen. It seeks to introduce stability to a poetic form too often seen as the exotic. As Agha Shahid Ali's editorship suggests, a ghazal swerves in the direction of a nostalgia that is forced to be proleptic. Here, formalism ceases to be simply structure and turns instead to the possibilities that form may allow. Certainly this experiment with the ghazal in English contains within it poems that appear to be shackled by an "alien" tradition. But the volume boldly declares that the boundaries of the exotic are inherently ephemeral, and that form itself questions the limitations of a specific cultural context and a specific language.

If ghazals can be written in American English, so be it. John Hollander's wonderful ghazal (cited in the introduction and produced in its entirety in the text) can serve as an ironic reminder of the possibility of formalism: His poem allows the reader to remain both amused and entranced by a metaphysical play of words that knows both its own stringency and its open-endedness. We do not have to rely on otherness, in other words, for the exotic to be translated into words that are incorporated into the contemporary and the immediate. The seeming alterity of the ghazal and its association with nineteenth-century Urdu poetry can indeed be adopted by an audience that signifies "today," or a poetic place that knows how difficult it is to become the landscape of home.

What then do we do with Mirza Asadullah Khan Ghalib, notwithstanding the anxiety of influence and similar superfluities? I must confess that I have not read an English translation of Ghalib that has pleased me—that has not made me angry—although I have spent some years being angered at my own attempts to do the same. A reader of Urdu must necessarily feel bereft at an inability of a language to embody the astonishment of the refrain that allows the publicity of repetition to occur simultaneously as an act of extreme privacy.

Ghalib and the privacy of desire—can that be available to translation? Perhaps. Are a *qafia* and a *radif* available for adoption? Maybe. Nothing could be quite so unusual as the notion of a refrain as a moment of secrecy. In Mirza Ghalib's poetry, however, the secret is made possible. It—and the cultural moment that surrounds the moment of poetry—may always remain untranslatable. There are poems in this collection that touch upon precisely that point of translation that converts a simple imitation of form into an opening, one that even Ghalib could admire. Cultural transitions take place.

The editor of the poems that we are asked to read is among the most subtle poets I have read in the United States today. He is, of course, a poet obsessed with form, which surely both licenses and explains his need to convert the ghazal into a medium available and most creatively useful to the poets of America in the present age. Perhaps he could preface this work by a quotation, and a wiser translation, of Ghalib: "There is a wilderness within a wilderness. / I saw the desert and remembered home."

Ideas of order suggest that there is no home in which form can locate its authenticity, that it indeed must travel and recreate its boundaries, however fragile they may be. The blessed rage for order does dictate the ghazal both in its parental and adoptive languages; we are privileged to read works of poetry that—as did the Ishmael of *Moby Dick*—found an orphan and called it home.

Sara Suleri Goodyear

.

Basic Points about the Ghazal

1. A ghazal is a poem of five to twelve couplets.

2. It contains no enjambments between couplets. Think of each couplet as a separate poem, in which the first line serves the function of the octave of a Petrarchan sonnet and the second line the sestet. That is, there must be a turn, a volta, when one moves from line 1 to line 2 of a couplet. Thus, certain kinds of enjambments would not work even WITHIN the couplets, the kind that would lead to a caesura in line 2. One must have a sense that line 2 is amplifying line 1, turning things around, surprising us.

3. Once again, there are ABSOLUTELY no enjambments between couplets. Each couplet must be like a precious stone that can shine even when plucked from the necklace, though it certainly has greater lustre in its setting.

4. What links these couplets is a strict formal scheme (I am talking of the canonical form of the ghazal, shaped by the Persians in, I believe, the eleventh century). This is how it works: The entire ghazal employs the SAME rhyme plus a refrain. THE RHYME MUST IMMEDIATELY PRECEDE THE REFRAIN. If the rhyme is merely buried somewhere in the line, that will have its charm, of course, but it would not lead to the wonderful pleasure of IMMEDIATE recognition which is central to the ghazal.

5. Each line must be of the same length (inclusive of the rhyme and refrain). In Urdu and Persian, all the lines are usually in the same meter and have the same metrical length. SO PLEASE ESTABLISH some system—metrical or syllabic—for maintaining consistency in line lengths.

6. The last couplet may be (and usually is) a signature couplet in which the poet may invoke his/her name in the first, second, or third person.

7. The scheme of rhyme and refrain occurs in BOTH lines of the first couplet (THAT IS HOW ONE LEARNS WHAT THE SCHEME IS) and then ONLY in the second line of every succeeding couplet (that is, the first line of every succeeding couplet may be anything as long as it maintains the syllabic or metrical length).

8. There is an epigrammatic terseness in the ghazal, but with immense lyricism, evocation, sorrow, heartbreak, wit. What defines the ghazal is a constant longing.

9. This is what a ghazal looks like:

Couplet one:

———————————————— rhyme A + refrain
———————————————— rhyme A + refrain

Couplet two:

————————————————————————
———————————————— rhyme A + refrain

Couplet three and so on:

————————————————————————
———————————————— rhyme A + refrain

THE REFRAIN MAY BE A WORD OR A PHRASE. (If it is a prepositional phrase, given the temperament of English, it may be acceptable to change the preposition. For example, if the preposition is "at the end," it should be all right to have "in the end," "to the end," and so on.)

10. Here are some opening and concluding couplets of mine:

Example A:

I say *That, after all, is the trick of it all*
When suddenly you say, "Arabic of it all."

For Shahid too the night went quickly as it came.
After that, O friend, came the music of it all.

Example B:

What will suffice for a true love knot? Even the rain?
But he has bought grief's lottery, bought even the rain.

They've found the knife that killed you, but whose prints are these?
No one has such small hands, Shahid, not even the rain.

Example C:

Suspended in the garden, Time, bit by bit, shines—
As you lean over this page, late and alone, it shines.

Mark how Shahid returns your very words to you.
It's when the heart, still unbriefed, but briefly lit, shines.

Example D:

Where are you now? Who lies beneath your spell tonight
before you agonize him in farewell tonight?

And I, Shahid, only am escaped to tell thee—
God sobs in my arms. Call me Ishmael tonight.

Notes on Contributors

Diane Ackerman is the author of seventeen works of poetry and nonfiction, including most recently *Deep Play* (prose) and *I Praise My Destroyer* (poetry). In addition to her literary honors, she has the somewhat unusual distinction of having a molecule named after her.

Sondra Audin Armer's published poems include more than a dozen in formal verse: sonnet, blank verse, pantoum, couplets, syllabics, nonce forms, and quatrains, one of which is included in the anthology *Dog Music: Poetry About Dogs*. This is her first ghazal in print.

Craig Arnold's first book, *Shells*, was the 1999 volume of the Yale Series of Younger Poets. He lives in Salt Lake City.

Diane Averill's two full-length books, *Branches Doubled Over With Fruit* and *Beautiful Obstacles* were both finalists for the Oregon Book Award. She received a 1999 Oregon Literary Arts Fellowship in poetry.

John Balaban's ghazal is the last poem in his prize-winning *Locusts at the Edge of Summer: New and Selected Poems*. He is Poet-in-Residence at North Carolina State University in Raleigh.

Carol Jane Bangs directed the Port Townsend Writers' Conference for sixteen years. A poet, essayist, fiction writer, she lives on an island in Puget Sound.

Molly Bendall's two collections of poems are *After Estrangement* and *Dark Summer*. She teaches at the University of Southern California.

Lorna Knowles Blake is a poet and translator who lives and works in New York City. Her poems have recently appeared in the journal *Pivot* and in the anthology *Ice: New Writing on Hockey*, edited by Dale Jacobs. She is currently in the M.F.A. program in writing at Sarah Lawrence College.

Robert Boswell is the author of six books of fiction, including *American Owned Love, Living to Be 100*, and *Mystery Ride*. His awards include the 1995 PEN West

Award for Fiction, and the 1996 Evil Companions Award. He teaches at New Mexico State University and in the Warren Wilson M.F.A. Program for Writers.

Karen Brennan's first book of poetry was *Here On Earth*. She won the AWP short fiction prize for her collection *Wild Desire*. Her memoir, *Rachel's Journey* is forthcoming. She is an associate professor at the University of Utah and teaches regularly at the Warren Wilson M.F.A. Program for Writers.

Sharon Bryan's most recent book of poems is *Flying Blind*. She is also the editor of *Where We Stand: Women Poets on Literary Tradition*.

Denver Butson's books include *Triptych* and *Mechanical Birds*. He teaches for his own writers' studio, WritersWriting, in New York City.

John Canaday is a winner of the New Millennium Poetry Award, and his poems have appeared or are forthcoming in among such journals as *The Paris Review*, *Raritan*, and *New England Review*. He is also the author of *The Nuclear Muse: Literature, Physics, and the First Atomic Bombs*.

Robert N. Casper is the publisher of *Jubilat*. He lives in Cambridge, Massachusetts.

G. S. Sharat Chandra has been teaching creative writing in America for the last thirty years. He's well known internationally for his poetry and fiction. In 1993, he published *Immigrants of Loss* and *Family of Mirrors*. *Sari of the Gods* appeared in 1998.

Richard Chess is an associate professor of literature and language at the University of North Carolina at Asheville. He directs UNCA's Center for Jewish Studies. He has published one book of poetry, *Tekiah*, and his poems have been anthologized in *Telling and Remembering: A Century of American-Jewish Poetry*.

Marcyn Del Clements's poetry has been published in *Alaska Quarterly Review*, *Appalachia, Eureka Literary Magazine, Flyway, frogpond, Hollins Critic, Literary Review, Lyric, Sijo West, Snowy West, Snowy Egret, Wind*, and *Yankee Magazine*.

Katherine Coles's third collection of poems, *The Golden Years of the Fourth Dimension*, will be published in 2001. Her previous books include *History of the Garden* (poems) and *The Measurable World* (a novel). Coles directs and teaches in the creative writing program at the University of Utah.

Michael Collier directs the Bread Loaf Writers' Conference as well as the M.F.A. Program in Creative Writing at the University of Maryland. His most recent book of poems is *The Ledge*.

Martha Collins's fourth book of poems, *Some Things Words Can Do*, was published in 1998. She is Pauline Delaney Professor of Creative Writing at Oberlin College, where she also serves as an editor of *FIELD*.

Steven Cordova has poems in *Barrow Street, Callaloo, The Journal* and *Puerto Del Sol*. He was born and raised in San Antonio, Texas and lives in New York City.

Katherine Cottle received her M.F.A. in creative writing from the University of Maryland at College Park. She has been published in *Puerto del Sol, Willow Springs, The Greensboro Review*, and various other literary magazines.

Rachel Dacus's poetry and essays have appeared in a wide range of print and on-line magazines, including *The Alsop Review, The Bitter Oleander, Conspire, Midwest Quarterly, Poet Lore,* and *Switched-On Gutenberg*. Her books include *Earth Lessons* and *Pavements of San Pedro*, a novel of place in verse and prose.

Keki N. Daruwalla has published seven volumes of poetry, a novella, and two volumes of short stories. His volume *Landscapes* won the Commonwealth Poetry Prize (Asia Region) in 1987.

Sharon Dolin is the author of a book of poems, *Heart Work*, and two chapbooks, *Mistakes* and *Climbing Mount Sinai*. She teaches poetry workshops at the 92nd Street Y Unterberg Poetry Center and at The School in New York City.

John Drury is the author of *The Disappearing Town* (2000) and *The Poetry Dictionary* (1995). He teaches at the University of Cincinnati.

Faiz Ahmed Faiz (1911–1984) is considered one of the two greatest Urdu poets of the twentieth century.

Annie Finch's books of poetry include *Eve* and *Marie Moving*. She has also edited many books on poetics, most recently *An Exaltation of Forms: Contemporary Poets Celebrate Diversity of Their Art*. Her website is at muohio.edu/~finchar.

Forrest Gander is the author of several books of poems and translations, including *Science & Steepleflower*. He teaches at Harvard University.

Mirza Asadullah Khan Ghalib (1797–1864) is to Urdu what Shakespeare is to English and Dante is to Italian.

Reginald Gibbons is the author of six books of poetry, most recently *Sparrow: New and Selected Poems* and *Homage to Longshot O'Leary*. He has also translated Euripides' *Bakkhai*, and published works of fiction.

Justin Goldberg is currently a junior at Princeton University, studying in the English and Creative Writing departments. He is originally from Baltimore, Maryland.

Sara Suleri Goodyear is a professor of English at Yale University. She is the author of *Meatless Days* and *The Rhetoric of English India*.

John Gribble's poems have appeared in *Pearl*, *The Mayland Poetry Review*, *Printed Matter*, and other publications in the United States, Japan, and Great Britain. A Southern California native, he now lives and teaches in Tokyo.

John Haag served on Merchant ships in WWII, and in the United States Navy during the Korean War. He taught poetry at Penn State from 1961 until 1994. His books include *The Mirrored Man*, *The Brine Breather*, and *Stones Don't Float*.

Marilyn Hacker is the author of nine books, most recently *Squares and Courtyards*, as well as the verse novel *Love, Death, and the Changing of the Seasons*. She lives in New York City and Paris, and is the director of the Graduate Program in English and Creative Writing at the City College of New York.

Daniel Hales teaches English and Creative Writing at The New Directions School in Northampton, Massachusetts. He holds an M.F.A. in Poetry Writing from the University of Massachsetts at Amherst. He's had poems appear recently in *Paragraph*, *Key Satch(el)*, *Ixnay*, and *Topic*.

Daniel Hall is the author of two books of poems, *Hermit with Landscape* and *Strange Relation*.

Robert Hastings was in his early teens when he sent in his ghazal. Now in his mid-teens, he is still the youngest contributor to the anthology. He lives in Chicopee, Massachusetts.

Christian Hawkey lives in Ashfield, Massachusetts.

James Heflin was born in Texas and lives in Montague, Massachusetts. He holds a M.F.A. from the University of Massachusetts at Amherst. He writes fiction and poetry and plays in the experimental rock band Down All the Days.

Cynthia Hogue's new collection is *The Never Wife*. She directs the Stadler Center for Poetry at Bucknell University.

John Hollander is Sterling Professor at Yale. His first volume, *A Crackling of Thorns*, was chosen by W. H. Auden for the Yale Series of Younger Poets. One of this country's most distinguished literary figures, he has published seventeen collections and many other editions and critical works. He has been awarded the Bollingen Prize in Poetry, as well as a MacArthur Fellowship.

Colette Inez has published eight books of poetry and has won Guggenheim, Rockefeller, and two NEA fellowships. She is widely anthologized and teaches at Columbia University's Writing Program.

David Raphael Israel established Ardeo as his poet's-name at age twelve, revived the sobriquet (as Raphael Ardeo) writing new-music journalism in his twenties, and again repaired to the *nom-de-plume* when dabbling in *ghazal*-writing in his thirties. If his poems appear sporadically, his paintings are seen more rarely.

James Jack is an air traffic controller in the United States Air Force. He, his wife, and their two sons are currently residing in Okinawa, Japan.

Shelli Jankowski-Smith's work has appeared in such publications as *Agni*, the *Boston Globe*, *CrossCurrents* and the *Harvard Review*, and she is co-editor of the anthology *In My Life: Encounters with the Beatles*. She was awarded a 1999 Coolidge Fellowship at Columbia by the Association for Religion and Intellectual Life, for her research in mystical poetry as a tool in interfaith dialogue.

Paul Jenkins is the author of *Forget the Sky*, *Radio Tooth*, and *Six Small Fires*. He teaches poetry and poetry writing at Hampshire College and is an editor of *The Massachusetts Review*.

Aaron Van Jordan is a graduate of the M.F.A. Program for Writers at Warren Wilson College, where he currently teaches in the undergraduate Writing Department as the 1999–2001 Joan Beebe Graduate Teaching Fellow.

Bhagwan Kapoor, based in New York, is a renowned professional artist and writes poetry. His poems have been featured in the Riverside Library Workshop anthologies and magazines in India. He has published limited editions of poems with original artwork.

Rafiq Kathwari, who deals in decorative crewel fabric from Kashmir, obtained an M.A. in Political Science from the New School for Social Research and a M.F.A. in Creative Writing from Columbia University, where he translated poems of Sir Iqbal.

Richard Kenney is the author of three books of poems: *The Evolution of the Flightless Bird*, *Orrery*, and *The Invention of Zero*. He lives in Port Townsend on the Olympic Peninsula and teaches at the University of Washington.

189

Nancy King has had two chapbooks published: *Traveling* and *Under This Roof.*

Phyllis Koestenbaum's publications include poems in two volumes of *The Best American Poetry, A Formal Feeling Comes: Poems in Form by Contemporary Women, Epoch, Michigan Quarterly Review,* and *Verse. Criminal Sonnets* is her most recent book.

Maxine Kumin has published eleven books of poetry, five novels, and three collections of essays. She lives and writes on her farm in New Hampshire.

Anthony Lacavaro holds an M.F.A. from the University of Massachusetts at Amherst. His poems have appeared in *The Paris Review, Western Humanities Review,* and *The Alembic,* as well as an anthology of sports poems. He lives in Brooklyn, N.Y.

Dominic Le Fave is an artist and independent philosopher of religions. His poetry has appeared in *Exquisite Corpse* and *Southwestern Review.* His current interests include the lyric dimensions of seventeenth-century rationalism and classical Islam.

Kelly Le Fave's recent poems have appeared in *The Massachusetts Review, The Notre Dame Review,* and *Tin House.* She holds an M.F.A. from the University of Massachusetts at Amherst.

Gabrielle LeMay will receive her M.F.A. in poetry from Hunter College in 2001. Her work has appeared in *Confrontation, Journal of New Jersey Poets, Paterson Literary Review,* and *River Oak Review,* and on *Wise Women's Web.*

Stuart Lishan is a member of the English Department of The Ohio State University, and his work has appeared in *Arts & Letters, The Kenyon Review, American Literary Review, Smartish Pace,* and other journals.

Barbara Little lives in Frederick, Maryland. She finds essential similarities between archaeology and poetry, making her living at the former and sustaining it with the latter. Her work has appeared in *The MacGuffin, The Plastic Tower,* and local publications.

William Matthews (1942–1997) received the National Book Critics Circle Award in Poetry for his tenth volume, *Time & Money,* and, in 1997, the Ruth Lilly Award from the Modern Poetry Association. His other volumes of poetry include *A Happy Childhood* (1984), *Blues if You Want* (1989), and *After All: Last Poems* (1998).

Glyn Maxwell, of Hertfordshire, England, is currently Visiting Writer at Amherst College. His most recent book is *Time's Fool*.

J. D. McClatchy is a distinguished author and critic. His most recent books include *Twenty Questions* and *Ten Commandments*. His collection of literary essays, *White Paper*, was given the Melville Cane Award by the Poetry Society of America. Since 1991, he has served as editor of *The Yale Review*.

Andrew McCord's poetry and translations have appeared in various magazines, including the Paris and Yale reviews, *Conjunctions*, *Grand Street*, and *Modern Poetry in Translation*.

Heather McHugh is Millman Distinguished Writer-in-Residence and Professor of English at the University of Washington in Seattle. She also regularly teaches in the M.F.A. Program for Writers at Warren Wilson college. Her six books of poetry include *Hinge & Sign: Poems, 1968–1993* and *The Father of the Predicaments*.

W. S. Merwin has won the Pulitzer Prize in Poetry, the Bollingen Prize in Poetry, the Fellowship of the Academy of American Poets, and the Tanning Prize for mastery in the art of poetry. His first book, *A Mask for Janus*, was chosen by W. H. Auden for the Yale Younger Poets Series in 1952. His most recent books of poetry are *The Folding Cliffs*; *The River Sound*; and *Purgatorio*, a translation from Dante.

Padmini Mongia teaches English literature at Franklin & Marshall College. An occasional poet, she has published articles on Joseph Conrad, Indian fiction, and has edited *Contemporary Postcolonial Theory: A Reader*.

Paul Muldoon, who was born in Ireland in 1951, now lives and teaches in Princeton, New Jersey. He is Professor of Poetry at the University of Oxford.

Isabel Nathaniel's book, *The Dominion of Lights*, won the Texas Institute of Letters poetry award. She is the recipient of a *Discovery/The Nation* prize and five Poetry Society of America awards.

Mil Norman-Risch is enrolled in Middlebury's Bread Loaf School of English and teaches at a private high school in Richmond, Virginia. She is co-author of a humanities textbook.

Peggy O'Brien's poems have appeared in journals both in this country and in Ireland. A member of the English Department at the University of Massachusetts, she is a frequent essayist on contemporary Irish poetry and editor of the *Wake Forest Book of Irish Women's Poetry: 1967–2000*.

James O'Keefe has a law degree from Harvard and an M.F.A. from the University of Maryland. His manuscript, Muscle, languishes in a desk drawer in Maine.

Jacqueline Osherow's fourth book of poetry is *Dead Men's Praise*. She has been a recipient of Guggenheim, NEA and Ingram Merrill fellowships, as well as the Witter Bynner Prize from the American Academy and Institute of Arts and Letters.

Elise Paschen is Director of the Poetry Society of America. She holds a Ph.D. in English from Oxford, where she wrote her dissertation on Yeats. Her first collection, *Infidelities,* received the Nicholas Roerich Poetry Prize. Her work has been published in numerous anthologies and magazines, including *Poetry, The New Yorker*, and *The New Republic*.

Peg Peoples's poems have appeared in *River Styx, New Letters,* and elsewhere. Currently she is director of Alice James Books and teaches at the University of Farmington at Maine.

Teresa M. Pfeifer lives and wonders in western Massachusetts.

Stanley Plumly's latest book is *Now that My father Lies Down Beside Me: New & Selected Poems, 1970-2000*. He is a Distinguished University Professor at the University of Maryland.

Mary Pryor writes in Moorhead, Minnesota, where she retired in 1992 from the English Department of Moorhead State University. She is the author of *On Occasion, Selected Poems, 1968-1992*.

John Richard Reed has appeared in *Poetry* and the *Paris Review*, among other journals. A student at San Francisco Theological Seminary, he is also represented in *Ten Poets*.

Mary Jo Salter is the author of four books of poems, most recently *A Kiss in Space*. She is Emily Dickinson Lecturer in the Humanities at Mount Holyoke College.

Grace Schulman's new book of poems is *The Paintings of Our Lives*. Her previous poetry collections include *For That Day Only, Hemispheres*, and *Burn Down the Icons*.

Sagaree Sengupta is a poet, scholar and translator currently teaching Hindi and Urdu at the University of Wisconsin, Madison. Her research focuses on nineteenth-century South Asian literature in its historical context; and she has translated Urdu, Bengali, and Hindi literature from various periods.

Greg Simon lives and works in Portland, Oregon. He is the co-translator, with Steven F. White and Christopher Maurer, of Federico Garcia Lorca's *Poet in New York* and the editor of *Heart of Darkness, Ferida Durakovic.*

Maurya Simon is the author of five volumes of poetry, including *Weavers*, a work created in collaboration with Los Angeles artist, Baila Goldenthal, and *A Brief History of Punctuation*. Simon is a professor in the Creative Writing Department at the University of California, Riverside.

David R. Slavitt is the author of more than seventy books of poetry, fiction, and translation. His recent volumes include *PS3569.L3, The Book of the Twelve Prophets, The Latin Odes of Jean Dorat*, and *The Sonnets of and Death of Jean de Sponde*. He is on the faculty of Bennington College.

Ron Smith is the author of *Running Again in Hollywood Cemetery* (poems). He is currently Writer-in-Residence at St. Christopher's School in Richmond, Virginia, where he also teaches creative writing in the University of Richmond's School of Continuing Studies. His work has recently been nominated for a Pushcart Prize and is included in the anthology *Georgia Voices.*

Carole Stone is an English Professor at Montclair State University. Her poetry books include *Orphan in the Movie House* and *Lime and Salt*. She received three fellowships from the New Jersey State Council on the Arts.

Elisabeth Stoner lives and writes outside rural West Grove, Pennsylvania.

Adrienne Su is the author of *Middle Kingdom*, a book of poems, and visiting poet-in-residence at Dickinson College, 2000–01.

Dorothea Tanning was born in Galesburg, Illinois. She is a painter, sculptor, and writer. That is, she is an artist who also writes: essays, fiction, poems and, most recently, a memoir, *Between Lives*. She has lived in Chicago, New York, Arizona, and for twenty-eight years, in France, returning to the United States in 1979. Tanning is one of this country's most distinguished Expressionists. She lives in New York City.

Judith Taylor is the author of a book of poems, *Curios*. She is the recipient of a Pushcart Prize.

Jennifer Tonge's poems have appeared in such journals as *Poetry, The New England Review,* and *Ploughshares*. She has also contributed entries to Routledge's *Who's Who in 20th Century World Poetry.*

Roderick Townley is the author of ten books, including a novel, several volumes of poetry, three nonfiction books, and a forthcoming children's book, *The Great Good Thing*. Winner of the Peregrine Prize in short fiction, he recently edited the anthology *Night Errands: How Poets Use Dreams*.

Wyatt Townley lives in Kansas. Her work has appeared in magazines ranging from *The Paris Review* to *Newsweek*, and her first book *Perfectly Normal* was a finalist in the Yale Series of Younger Poets.

Ann Townsend's first collection of poetry, *Dime Store Erotics,* was published in 1998. Her poems, stories, and essays have appeared in *Poetry, The Paris Review, The Nation,* and elsewhere. She teaches at Denison University in Granville, Ohio, where she also directs the Jonathan R. Reynolds Young Writers Workshop.

Ellen Bryant Voigt is the author of five volumes of poetry—*Claiming Kin*, *The Forces of Plenty*, *The Lotus Flower*, *Two Trees*, and *Kyrie*, a National Book Critics Circle Award Finalist—and a collection of craft essays, *The Flexible Lyric*. She teaches in the Warren Wilson College low-residency M.F.A. Program for Writers and is currently the Vermont State Poet.

Bryan Walpert received his M.F.A. at the University of Maryland and is now in the Ph.D program in English at the University of Denver, where he teaches writing. His poems have appeared or are forthcoming in *Crab Orchard Review*, *The Lyric*, *The Metropolitan Review,* and *Poet Lore*.

Rosanna Warren is the Emma MacLachlan Metcalf Professor of the Humanities at Boston University. Her most recent book of poems, *Stained Glass*, won the Lamont Prize from the Academy of American Poets.

Robert William Watkins is a young Canadian poet. He is currently putting the "finishing touches" on *What Canada's All About and Other Ghazals*.

Ellen Doré Watson, poet and translator, is the author of *We Live in Bodies* and the translator of a dozen books from Brazilian Portuguese, including *The Alphabet in the Park: Selected Poems of Adélia Prado*. Watson is director of the Poetry Center at Smith College, and serves as an editor at *The Massachusetts Review*.

Paul West's forty-odd books most recently include *O.K.*, a novel about Doc Holliday; *The Dry Danube*, a novella about Hitler as a failed artist; and *The Secret Lives of Words*, a work of licentious etymology. The government of France recently created him a Chevalier of the Order of Arts and Letters.

Rachel Wetzsteon is the author of two books of poems, *The Other Stars* and *Home and Away*.

John Edgar Wideman, a 1966 graduate of Oxford University, is the second African-American Rhodes Scholar. He is presently a full professor of creative writing at the University of Massachusetts at Amherst and a two-time Pen/Faulkner Award winner, as well as a recipient of the MacArthur Prize fellowship (1994). His published works include *A Glance Away* (1967), *Hurry Home* (1970), *The Lynchers* (1973), *The Homewood Trilogy* (*Damballah* [1981], *Hiding Place* [1981], *Sent for You Yesterday* [1983]), *Brothers and Keepers* (1984), *Rueben* (1987), *Fever* (1989), *Philadelphia Fire* (1990), *All Stories are True* (1992), *Father Along* (1994), *The Cattle Killing* (1996), and *Two Cities* (1998).

Bruce Williams grew up in Denver, was educated at Grinnell College, UCLA, and Claremont Graduate School, and teaches writing and literature at Mt. San Antonio College, east of Los Angeles. His work has appeared in *Solo, California Quarterly, The American Indian Culture and Research Journal*, and more recently in *Holistic Dressing: Clothes Poems and Other Obsessions* and *Stratification*.

Eleanor Wilner's most recent books of poetry are *Reversing the Spell: New and Selected Poems* and *Otherwise*. She teaches in the M.F.A. Program for Writers at Warren Wilson College.

Stephen Yenser's books include *The Fire in All Things*, which received the Walt Whitman Award from the Academy of American Poets. He is Professor of English and Director of Creative Writing at UCLA.

David Young's new and selected poems, *The Planet on the Desk*, was published in 1990. He is also the author of *Night Thoughts and Henry Vaughan*, *Seasoning: A Poet's Year*, and *At the White Window*.

Harriet Zinnes is Professor emerita of English of Queens College of the CUNY. Her many books include *My, Haven't the Flowers Been?* (poems), *The Radiant Absurdity of Desire* (short stories), *Ezra Pound and the Visual Arts* (criticism), and *Blood and Feathers*, translations from the French poetry of Jacques Prevert. She is a contributing editor of *The Hollins Critic* and a contributing writer of *New York Arts Magazine*.

Martha Zweig, recipient of a 1999 Whiting Writer's Award, is the author of *Vinegar Bone* and *Powers*. Her poems appear widely, including another ghazal in *American Literary Review*.

About the Editor

Agha Shahid Ali, on the poetry faculty of the M.F.A./Ph.D Program in Creative Writing at the University of Utah as well as the M.F.A. Program for Writers at Warren Wilson College, has held visiting appointments at State University of New York-Binghamton, Princeton, and New York University and taught formerly at Hamilton College and the University of Massachusetts at Amherst. His seven collections of poetry include *The Half-Inch Himalayas* (Wesleyan University Press), *A Walk Through the Yellow Pages* (SUN/gemini Press), *A Nostalgist's Map of America* (W. W. Norton), *The Belovéd Witness: Selected Poems* (Viking Penquin), and—most recently—*The Country Without a Post Office* (W. W. Norton), a collection that focuses on the turmoil in Kashmir, where he is from originally and where he spends his summers. He is also the translator of *The Rebel's Silhouette: Selected Poems* by Faiz Ahmed Faiz (University of Massachusetts Press, revised edition) as well as the author of *T. S. Eliot as Editor* (University of Michigan Research Press). His poems appear regularly in journals such as *Antioch Review*, *Chelsea*, *Denver Quarterly*, *Field*, *Grand Street*, *London Magazine*, *The Nation*, *Paris Review*, *Poetry*, *Tri-Quarterly*, and *Yale Review*. A recipient of Guggenheim and Ingram Merrill fellowships, he has also won fellowships from the Pennsylvania Council on the Arts, the Breadloaf Writers' Conference, and the New York Foundation for the Arts—as well as a Pushcart Prize.